The HOLY GHOST

The HOLY GHOST

Joseph Fielding McConkie
Robert L. Millet

BOOKCRAFT
Salt Lake City, Utah

Library of Congress Catalog Card Number: 89-62190

ISBN 0-88494-707-6

4th Printing, 1993

Printed in the United States of America

Dedicated to our grandfathers,
Oscar W. McConkie, Sr., and Anatole J. Millet,
two powerful preachers of righteousness from whom
we learned much about the operations of the Spirit

Without the aid of the Holy Ghost no man can know the will of God, or that Jesus is the Christ.

—Joseph F. Smith

Contents

Preface

When asked by Martin Van Buren, then the president of the United States, how Mormonism differed from other religions of the day, the Prophet Joseph Smith is reported to have said, "We [differ] in mode of baptism, and the gift of the Holy Ghost by the laying on of hands." All other considerations, the Prophet said, are "contained in the gift of the Holy Ghost." (*History of the Church*, 4:42.) The Prophet's statement suggests that the distinctive characteristic of the Lord's people—and this would be so in all generations of time—has been the companionship of the Holy Ghost and the attendant manifestation of the gifts of the Spirit. Where that gift and its fruits are found, there the truths and authority of salvation are found; where that gift and its attendant fruits are not found, there the church and kingdom of God are yet to be established.

If a people have the gift of the Holy Ghost, of necessity they also have the higher or holy priesthood, the authority to administer the gospel, the key to unlock the mysteries of the kingdom of heaven, and power to commune with and enjoy the presence of God and angels (see D&C 84:19; 107:18–19). Indeed, "no man can receive the Holy Ghost," Joseph Smith taught, "without receiving revelations" (*Teachings of the Prophet Joseph Smith*, p. 328). A people who have the Holy Ghost will of necessity have the spirit of prophecy and revelation also. They will profess not only the right but the responsibility to add to the canon of scripture, and they will maintain that it is not only the privilege but the responsibility of all to whom this sacred gift has been given to receive personal revelation.

The Holy Ghost is as the breath of life to the Church. It is the source of all truth and spiritual knowledge. In the kingdom of God there are no doctrines that do not bear the label of divine revelation and thus the handprint of the Holy Ghost. Independent of the Holy Ghost, we are without the right to teach the gospel and without the capacity to learn it. As to the spirit that is to sustain those who teach the gospel, revelation declares that they are to "speak as they are moved upon by the Holy Ghost. And whatsoever they shall speak when moved upon by the Holy Ghost shall be scripture, shall be the will of the Lord, shall be the mind of the Lord, shall be the word of the Lord, shall be the voice of the Lord, and the power of God unto salvation." (D&C 68:3-4.)

There are no words equal to the task of describing the gratitude that ought be ours toward that God who gave us life. That same Lord has provided the means whereby we might be redeemed from the effects of Adam's fall and has also granted us the right to enjoy the companionship of the Holy Ghost. "There is no doubt," observed Brigham Young, "if a person lives according to the revelations given to God's people, he may have the Spirit of the Lord to signify to him His will, and to guide and to direct him in the discharge of his duties, in his temporal as well as his spiritual exercises. I am satisfied, however, that in this respect, we live far beneath our privileges." (*Journal of Discourses*, 12:104.)

"For what doth it profit a man if a gift is bestowed upon him, and he receive not the gift? Behold, he rejoices not in that which is given unto him, neither rejoices in him who is the giver of the gift." (D&C 88:33.) For Latter-day Saints to be unmindful of the command that we seek and in reality "receive the Holy Ghost" is to fail to reverence God, from whom that supernal gift is given, and to deny ourselves access to those enlightening and sanctifying powers of the Spirit which feed the soul. It is to hunger and thirst when the bread of life and living waters are within reach; to stand naked before the world when we could have been clothed with the dignity, power, and authority from on high; to be tainted and soiled when we could enjoy the consummate peace of personal purity. We have written in the hope of stimulating faith, of creating interest, and of extending encouragement, that in the realm of spiritual things the confidence of the Latter-day Saints might wax strong in the presence of God. Such has been the effect upon our own souls in the preparation of this work, for which we properly assume responsibility.

The Holy Ghost invites us to step beyond the boundary drawn to guard the sanctity of Sinai, to purify ourselves, and to ascend the holy mountain that we might stand in the divine presence. In-

deed, eye hath not seen nor ear heard of the marvels God has prepared for those of the house of faith, "neither is man capable to
make them known, for they are only to be seen and understood by
the power of the Holy Spirit, which God bestows on those who love
him, and purify themselves before him; to whom he grants this
privilege of seeing and knowing for themselves; that through the
power and manifestation of the Spirit, while in the flesh, they may
be able to bear his presence in the world of glory" (D&C 76:116–
18).

1

The Ministry of the Holy Ghost

*When he, the Spirit of truth, is come, he will guide
you into all truth.*

—John 16:13

The spring of 1820 heralded the dawning of a brighter day.
Where for generations fear and doubt and superstition had
clouded men's minds, where deceit and error and mystery and
misunderstanding had characterized the religious teachings for
centuries, now love and light and pure religion became the order of
the day among those willing to accept and receive this modern revelation, this "new" religion. Whereas darkness had reigned, now
the rising of the gospel sun shed forth its rays of penetrating and
permeating light. The heavens had been rent, and men no longer
were required to exist on borrowed light. God had spoken anew.
He and his Beloved Son had appeared personally to a young man
in a grove made sacred by the occasion and had opened wide the
windows of heaven. In process of time the great God began to
make himself known to mortal man, to unfold those fundamental
and foundational truths concerning God and the Godhead which
provide purpose and perspective and parameters for all other doctrines.

The Restoration of Heavenly Powers

Within a hundred years after the death of Christ the gospel light which he had lit had begun to fade. With the deaths of those holding apostolic power, and with the incorporation of Greek philosophy into Christian theology and the hybrid heresies flowing therefrom, the long night of apostate darkness set in. True it is that centuries later good and noble men and women were raised up — "morning stars who shone more brightly than their fellows — who arose in every nation," persons "of insight and courage who were sickened by the sins and evils of the night. These great souls hacked and sawed at the chains with which the masses were bound. They sought to do good and to help their fellowmen — all according to the best light and knowledge they had." (Bruce R. McConkie, Conference Report, April 1978, p. 17.) People of such fortitude prepared the way for the Restoration by helping to bring to pass the Reformation; and centuries later others of like spiritual propensity followed the promptings and guidance of Providence in their quest for personal and religious freedoms and thereby led the way in the establishment of the American nation, the nation foreordained as the land in which the marvelous work and a wonder was to be brought forth.

And yet amid it all, the gift of the Holy Ghost — that sacred grace which entitles the Saints of all ages to enjoy the constant companionship of a member of the Godhead and thus to bask in the light of heaven — was not to be found on earth. Joseph Smith came into a world where people of all walks of life were seeking light and truth, yearning for that inspiration which had animated the souls of the ancients. Sincerity abounded, but ignorance and misunderstanding were the order of the day. As the Prophet of the Restoration would later observe: "Various and conflicting are the opinions of men in regard to the gift of the Holy Ghost. . . . It is not to be wondered at that men should be ignorant, in a great measure, of the principles of salvation, and more especially of the nature, office, power, influence, gifts and blessings of the Gift of the Holy Ghost; when we consider that the human family have been enveloped in gross darkness and ignorance for many centuries past without revelation, or any just criterion to arrive at a knowledge of the things of God, which can only be known by the spirit of God.'' (*Times and Seasons*, 3:823.)

Before the God of heaven could fully bring to pass the work of restoration—a work which was destined to continue into the days of millennial splendor—it was necessary that he restore those powers and authorities that had been enjoyed by the ancients. Before there could be a church there must first be authority to organize it. Before the everlasting gospel could shed its glorious rays of light upon a people who had been walking in darkness for centuries, there must first be a priesthood to administer that gospel.

And so it was that early, very early in the formative period of the Church's history, God restored those priesthoods and keys by which men could serve as agents—could act and speak on behalf of the Lord Jesus, who was their eternal principal. On 15 May 1829 an angel of God descended from the courts of glory, laid his hands upon the heads of Joseph Smith and Oliver Cowdery, ordained them priests of the ancient order of Aaron, and empowered them to officiate in ''outward ordinances, the letter of the gospel, the baptism of repentance for the remission of sins'' (D&C 107:20; *Teachings of the Prophet Joseph Smith*, p. 335). John the Baptist, a literal descendant of Aaron himself and the man in time's meridian entitled to the office we know today as Presiding Bishop, conferred the rights of presidency pertaining to the Aaronic Priesthood, thereby entitling men once again to hold ''the key of the ministering of angels and the preparatory gospel'' (D&C 84:26), including the power to perform authorized baptisms by water.

Within a matter of weeks, Peter, James, and John—the First Presidency of the dispensation of the meridian of time—restored those priesthood powers whose keys entitle faithful men to hold communion with the heavens, a priesthood which ''administereth the gospel and holdeth the key of the mysteries of the kingdom, even the key of the knowledge of God'' (D&C 84:19). The power of this higher or Melchizedek Priesthood ''is to hold the keys of all the spiritual blessings of the church—to have the privilege of receiving the mysteries of the kingdom of heaven, to have the heavens opened unto them, to commune with the general assembly and church of the Firstborn, and to enjoy the communion and presence of God the Father, and Jesus the mediator of the new covenant'' (D&C 107:18-19). And with the restoration of the holy priesthood came the supernal power to bestow the gift of the Holy Ghost, power to confirm individuals members of the Lord's Church, power to consummate the baptism of water and bring to pass that second baptism called in scripture the baptism of fire, that immersion in the heavenly element which purifies and cleanses the human soul and prepares the initiate to receive knowledge of transcendent realities.

The Gift of the Holy Ghost

Eternal life is the greatest of all the gifts of God (D&C 6:13; 14:7; 1 Nephi 15:36), but it is a gift which is realized fully only in eternity. In this life there is a gift which is more precious than all the wealth and honor and applause that men can bestow, a gift whose effects are grander and more profound than all the knowledge that can be gained at the feet of the most learned of the day. It is the gift of the Holy Ghost. It is a gift which may not be purchased with money nor bartered for with this world's goods. It is granted by a loving Father in Heaven to those who accept and exercise faith in Christ the Lord, repent of their sins, and are baptized by immersion by an ordained legal administrator. An account from the New Testament illustrates how the gift of the Holy Ghost is and is *not* to be had.

> Now when the apostles which were at Jerusalem heard that Samaria had received the word of God, they sent unto them Peter and John:
> Who, when they were come down, prayed for them, that they might receive the Holy Ghost:
> (For as yet he was fallen upon none of them: only they were baptized in the name of the Lord Jesus.)
> Then laid they their hands on them, and they received the Holy Ghost.
> And when Simon [Magus] saw that through laying on of the apostles' hands the Holy Ghost was given, he offered them money,

Saying, Give me also this power, that on whomsoever I lay hands, he may receive the Holy Ghost.

But Peter said unto him, Thy money perish with thee, because thou hast thought that the gift of God may be purchased with money. (Acts 8:14–20.)

This account from the early Christian Church teaches clearly that the receipt of the gifts of God—particularly the gift of the Holy Ghost—is to be had in the prescribed and ordained manner, or it is to be had not at all. Elder Jedediah M. Grant spoke of the absolute necessity for the Saints of God and for all people to have personal experience with the Spirit and not be satisfied with reading the accounts of others of the past. "When you read of the gifts that were bestowed upon and circulated among the people of God," he reminded us, "you certainly would not wish others to suppose that mere reading about them puts you in possession of the same blessings." He continued:

But many in the world would suppose that when they preach and circulate the Bible, they actually put in the possession of the people that power and life and those gifts, that the ancient Apostles and Prophets and Saints of God enjoyed.

Brethren and sisters, we understand the difference between enjoying and reading of enjoyment, between the history of a feast and the feast itself; also between the history of the law of God and the law itself.

When the Prophet Joseph came among the people he did not tell them that he would sell them the word of God, but after he had established the truth in their minds and they were baptized, he then laid his hands upon them that they might receive the gift of the Holy Ghost, for he had promised this, and they received the Holy Comforter and the same light, the same Spirit, the same power of God, and the same principles of eternal life; that very gift which is the greatest gift of God, and it gave them the same joy, and the same great blessings, and this Spirit taught them the will of God. (*Journal of Discourses*, 4:18.)

Every man or woman born into this world is born with what the scriptures call the Light of Christ or the Spirit of Jesus Christ (D&C 84:46; Moroni 7:16; John 1:9). The Light of Christ is the means by which the cosmos is ordered, the power and force by which the laws of nature exist and hold sway in the universe (see D&C 88:6–13). This same light is planted in the spirit of man by a benevolent God and serves as the source of reason and conscience and discernment. It is a moral monitoring device, a directing and guiding influence which will strive with men and women and lead them to do good and choose righteousness if they will but acknowledge and respond to the soft inner impressions of this light. According to Elder Bruce R. McConkie, the Light of Christ, "defies description and is beyond mortal comprehension. . . . It has neither shape nor form nor personality. It is not an entity nor a person nor a personage. It has no agency, does not act independently, and exists not to act but to be acted upon. . . . It is variously described as light and life and law and truth and power. . . . It is the power of God who sitteth upon his throne. It may be that it is also priesthood and faith and omnipotence, for these too are the power of God." (*A New Witness for the Articles of Faith,* p. 257.)

The revelations attest that "the Spirit [Light of Christ] giveth light to every man that cometh into the world; and the Spirit enlighteneth every man through the world, that hearkeneth to the voice of the Spirit. And every one that hearkeneth to the voice of the Spirit cometh unto God, even the Father. And the Father teacheth him of the covenant which he has renewed and confirmed upon you." (D&C 84:46–48.) That is to say, if men and women in the world will respond to the quiet promptings and subtle whisperings of the Spirit of Jesus Christ within them, they will be led, either in this life or the next, to that higher light of the Holy Ghost found only in the covenant gospel through membership in the Lord's Church. President Joseph F. Smith explained that this light "strives with the children of men, and will continue to strive with them, until it brings them to a knowledge of the truth and the possession of the greater light and testimony of the Holy Ghost" (*Gospel Doctrine,* pp. 67–68). Further, Elder McConkie has described the relationship of the Light of Christ to the Holy Ghost as follows:

The light of Christ (also called the Spirit of Christ and the Spirit of the Lord) is a light, a power, and an influence that . . . is everywhere present and accounts for the omnipresence of God. It is the agency of God's power and the law by which all things are governed. *It is also the agency used by the Holy Ghost to manifest truth and dispense spiritual gifts to many people at one and the same time.* For instance, it is as though the Holy Ghost, who is a personage of spirit, was broadcasting all truth throughout the whole universe all the time, using the light of Christ as the agency by which the message is delivered. But only those who attune their souls to the Holy Spirit receive the available revelation. It is in this way that the person of the Holy Ghost makes his influence felt in the heart of every righteous person at one and the same time. (*A New Witness for the Articles of Faith*, p. 70, italics added.)

As contrasted with the Light of Christ (which is innate, inborn, intuitional in nature, available to all, and strives with all), the gift of the Holy Ghost is available only to baptized members of the Lord's Church through the ordinance of the laying on of hands. Though the influence of the Holy Ghost may be felt by one who has not been baptized, such an influence is temporary and fleeting. Peter, for example, received a flash of spiritual insight in the form of testimony when he bore witness of his Messiah at Caesarea Philippi (Matthew 16:16–19). It was not, however, until after the day of Pentecost—when the Holy Ghost and his gifts were poured out upon the people in a marvelous and miraculous manner—that Peter and the other disciples became the tireless and undaunted witnesses of their Master that characterized a people who had truly been born of the Spirit.

"There is a difference," Joseph Smith taught, "between [the influence of] the Holy Ghost and the gift of the Holy Ghost. Cornelius [see Acts 10] received [the influence of] the Holy Ghost before he was baptized, which was the convincing power of God unto him of the truth of the Gospel, but he could not receive the gift of the Holy Ghost until after he was baptized. Had he not taken this sign or ordinance upon him, the Holy Ghost which convinced him of the truth of God, would have left him. Until he obeyed these ordinances and received the gift of the Holy Ghost, by the laying on of hands, according to the order of God, he could not have healed the sick or commanded an evil spirit to come out of a man, and it obey him." (*Teachings of the Prophet Joseph Smith*, p. 199.)

The Person and Powers of the Holy Ghost

The witness or testator, known also as the Holy Ghost, is a male personage of spirit. He is the third member of the Godhead, the minister of the Father and the Son, the means by which the children of God are instructed in the ways of God, by which they gain "the mind of Christ" (1 Corinthians 2:16). He possesses the mind of God and the attributes of the Almighty. As a distinct personage, the Holy Ghost can be in only one place at a time, and always will be in the form of a man; he cannot transform himself into any other form (see *Teachings of the Prophet Joseph Smith*, pp. 275–76). By means of the Light of Christ his sacred influence is able to be felt in an infinite number of places at once.

In 1843 the Prophet Joseph Smith explained that "the Father has a body of flesh and bones as tangible as man's; the Son also; but the Holy Ghost has not a body of flesh and bones, but is a personage of Spirit. Were it not so, the Holy Ghost could not dwell in us. A man may receive the Holy Ghost, and it may descend upon him and not tarry with him." (D&C 130:22–23.) What does it mean that the Holy Ghost can "dwell in us"? How can one personage dwell within another, even if the former is a spirit personage? "According to the eternal laws ordained by the Father," Elder Bruce R. McConkie has written of this phenomenon, "there are certain separate and distinct things to be done by a spirit member of the Godhead. He is to dwell, figuratively, in the faithful, and he is to speak to their spirits in a special and particular way, which he can do because he himself is a spirit." Further:

> Knowing as we do that the Holy Ghost is the Minister of the Father and the Son—appointed by them, because he is a spirit, to perform a specialized service for men—the meaning

of these passages becomes clear. No member of the Godhead dwells in us in the literal sense of the word, but all of them dwell in us figuratively to the extent that we are like them. If we have "the mind of Christ" (1 Corinthians 2:16), which we receive by the power of the Holy Ghost, then Christ dwells in us. If the love of God abides in our souls, which love is a gift of God that comes by the power of the Holy Ghost, then God dwells in us. In some way beyond our comprehension, all of this is possible by the power of the Holy Ghost. (*A New Witness for the Articles of Faith,* pp. 70, 271–72.)

In this dispensation very little has been revealed as to the personal identity of the Holy Ghost. According to an account of a sermon delivered by Joseph Smith on 27 August 1843 and as recorded by Franklin D. Richards, the Prophet explained that "the Holy Ghost is now in a state of probation which, if he should perform in righteousness, he may pass through the same or a similar course of things that the Son has" (*Words of Joseph Smith,* p. 245, capitalization and punctuation corrected). In an address delivered only eleven days before his death, the Prophet is reported to have taught that "the Holy Ghost is yet a spiritual body and waiting to take to himself a body as the Savior did, or as God did, or the Gods before them took bodies" (*Words of Joseph Smith,* p. 382, capitalization and punctuation modernized). Beyond these brief and fragmentary statements, discussions concerning this spirit man are speculative and unproductive.

Nephi wrote that his father saw sacred things in a vision and also spoke many eternal verities "by the power of the Holy Ghost, which power he received by faith on the Son of God." Nephi went on to explain that the Holy Ghost is "the gift of God unto all those who diligently seek [Christ]. . . . For he that diligently seeketh shall find; and the mysteries of God shall be unfolded unto them, by the power of the Holy Ghost, as well in these times as in times of old, and as well in times of old as in times to come; wherefore, the course of the Lord is one eternal round." (1 Nephi 10:17, 19.) The power to bestow the gift of the Holy Ghost—received first by father Adam; conferred upon his noble sons in course; lost during periods of apostasy and delivered afresh during eras of restoration—has been restored in our day through angelic ministrations.

The work of the Holy Ghost is vital. His assignment with man is multifaceted, his labors multifold. In the words of a modern prophet, President Spencer W. Kimball, "the Holy Ghost is a revelator. . . . He is a reminder and will bring to our remembrance the things which we have learned and which we need in the time thereof. He is an inspirer and will put words in our mouths, enlighten our understandings and direct our thoughts. He is a testifier . . . a teacher . . . a companion and will walk with us, inspiring us all along the way, guiding our footsteps, impeaching our weaknesses, strengthening our resolves, and revealing to us righteous aims and purposes." (*Teachings of Spencer W. Kimball,* p. 23.) In this book we shall speak of some of the many roles of the Holy Ghost. We shall speak of the Holy Ghost as a revelator, a comforter, a teacher, a discerner of souls, a sanctifier, an agent of the new birth, and a sealer. We shall come to appreciate how it is that the powers of the Holy Ghost constitute an organizing principle, a divine medium by which order and system come to exist among people and practices. This is illustrated beautifully by a lesson delivered to President Brigham Young by Joseph Smith after the latter's death. The Prophet Joseph appeared to Brigham Young and instructed his successor as follows:

> Tell the people to be humble and faithful, and be sure to keep the Spirit of the Lord and it will lead them right. Be careful and not turn away the small still voice; it will teach them what to do and where to go; it will yield the fruits of the kingdom. Tell the brethren to keep their hearts open to conviction, so that when the Holy Ghost comes to them, their hearts will be ready to receive it. They can tell the Spirit of the Lord from all other spirits; it will whisper peace and joy to their souls; it will take malice, hatred, strife and all evil from their hearts; and their whole desire will be to do good, bring forth righteousness and build up the kingdom of God. Tell the brethren if they will follow the Spirit of the Lord, they will go right. Be sure to tell the people to keep the Spirit of the Lord; and if they will, they will find themselves just as

they were organized by our Father in Heaven before they came into the world. Our Father in Heaven organized the human family, but they are all disorganized and in great confusion. (*Journal History*, 23 February 1847.)

Indeed, by means of the Holy Ghost men and women ground themselves in the truth, establish themselves in the faith of their ancient fathers, and chart and follow that course which leads to peace and happiness here and the fulness of joy and eternal reward hereafter.

Conclusion

One of the marvelous insights restored through the Prophet Joseph Smith is the knowledge that the gifts of God—specifically the gift of the Holy Ghost—did not have their origins in the meridian of time, but rather have been enjoyed by the faithful of all ages. Peter testified that "prophecy came not in old time by the will of man: but holy men of God spake as they were moved by the Holy Ghost" (2 Peter 1:21). Indeed, "the Spirit is the same, yesterday, today, and forever" (2 Nephi 2:4). It is but appropriate, then, that the God of heaven should reveal anew those principles by which the Saints can develop in spiritual graces, and in addition that he should make known those mysteries dealing with the person and powers and operations of the Holy Ghost. The keys of the Melchizedek Priesthood—delivered to the modern seer by angelic ministrants—open the door to the knowledge of God and more specifically transform the weak and simple into legal administrators and empower them to bestow the gift of the Holy Ghost upon the faithful. The gift of the Holy Ghost is a priceless possession, but one that may not be purchased with money; it is a pearl of great price, but one that may be found only through the channels the Lord has ordained.

2

The Spirit of Revelation Restored

*And it shall come to pass afterward, that I will pour
out my spirit upon all flesh; and your sons and your
daughters shall prophesy, your old men shall dream
dreams, your young men shall see visions: and also
upon the servants and upon the handmaids in those
days will I pour out my spirit.*

—Joel 2:28–29

When the spirit of revelation is lost, the knowledge of how it
comes is lost also. Thus we were blessed in the opening of this dispensation with a series of revelations intended to acquaint the children of men once again with that Spirit by which they are to come
to know God, and through which they are to seek the wisdom of
heaven. A prophet is first and foremost a teacher, and to the extent
of our knowledge, no prophet has ever done more to teach men
how they may obtain the spirit of revelation than Joseph Smith.
His having done so stands as the perfect evidence that he is indeed
a true servant of the Lord Jesus Christ and the great prophet of the
Restoration.

Revelations on the Spirit of Revelation

For the Prophet Joseph Smith, the heavens were an open book.
He gave our present world more scripture than any prophet of any
age. He preserved "more of the mind and will and voice of the
Lord than the total of the dozen most prolific prophetic penmen of
the past." Through the "gift and power of God" he gave us the

Book of Mormon, published many visions and revelations of his own in a compilation known as the Doctrine and Covenants, "revised and added to the King James Version of the Bible by the spirit of inspiration, doing more to perfect that volume of holy writ and to return it to its state of pristine perfection than any single person has ever done." (Bruce R. McConkie, Conference Report, April 1976, p. 142.) Joseph Smith was no novice when it came to the companionship of the Holy Ghost, the entertaining of angels, or the seeing of visions.

In a meeting held in October of 1831, Hyrum Smith called upon his brother to explain how the Book of Mormon was translated. Joseph responded "that it was not intended to tell the world all the particulars of the coming forth of the Book of Mormon." He observed that it "was not expedient" for him to relate such things. (*Far West Record,* p. 23, capitalization corrected.) The Lord had previously told Joseph that if people would not believe the book itself they would not be converted by a knowledge of the details of the process of its translation (D&C 5:7). Conversion was to come from the witness of the Spirit. There is a sense, a feel, a power associated with the doctrines of heaven that is not found in the philosophical musings of men. A passage common to the revelations announcing the coming forth of the Book of Mormon attested that the word of God was "quick and powerful, sharper than a two-edged sword, to the dividing asunder of both joints and marrow" (D&C 6:2; 11:2; 12:2; 14:2). The word of God is "quick," meaning "alive and active" (see New English Bible, Hebrews 4:12). The idea being suggested is that it does not come with the casual meandering of a brook but rather with the swiftness of an arrow. It has the power to expand the mind, enlighten the understanding, and give birth to faith. Such is its power that it penetrates the depths of the soul and lifts men above the swamps of carnality and worldliness to the heights of the holy mountain where they can see the visions of eternity.

Even before the Church was organized, the Lord established the fact that the spirit of conviction, that spirit which confirms truth, centers in the message rather than the messenger, in the word rather than the medium by which the word is conveyed. This is not to say that the Lord withheld all understanding as to how the

Book of Mormon was translated. To the contrary, we are taught much in the experience of Oliver Cowdery as he attempted to translate. Indeed, Oliver becomes a classic case study as to how the spirit of revelation functions. A series of revelations unfold the story of how he grew up in the knowledge of the Holy Ghost. They begin with his asking the Prophet to inquire of the Lord in his behalf through the Urim and Thummim, the ancient seeric device given him to translate the Book of Mormon. Oliver wanted a revelation. He wanted to make contact with the heavens.

The revelation Joseph Smith received must have been something of a surprise to Oliver: "As often as thou hast inquired," the Lord said, "thou hast received instruction of my Spirit." That is, "Oliver, every time you have inquired, I have responded." To evidence the fact, the Lord said, "If it had not been so, thou wouldst not have come to the place where thou art at this time. Behold, thou knowest that thou hast inquired of me and I did enlighten thy mind; and now I tell thee these things that thou mayest know that thou hast been enlightened by the Spirit of truth." (D&C 6:13–14.)

Thus Oliver was given a revelation to tell him that he had been receiving revelation. He obviously did not know how the answers to his prayers would come. Presumably, he expected some kind of euphoric or ecstatic experience. Yet we find the Lord reminding him of the "night that you cried unto me in your heart, that you might know concerning the truth of these things. Did I not speak peace to your mind concerning the matter? What greater witness can you have than from God?" (D&C 6:22–23.) It is not necessary that God raise his voice to answer prayers. The "still small voice" is just that, "still" and "small." The language of peace, as spoken by the Lord, embraces a sense of quiet confidence, comfort, and warmth. It is gentle and calm, amiable and sweet; it is temperate and kind; it is orderly and identified by happiness, joy, and feelings of love. That spirit had caused Oliver to savor the truths revealed to him and had provoked him to aid in the great drama of the coming forth of the Book of Mormon. Describing his desire to be involved in the translation of the Book of Mormon, Oliver observed that those feelings were so strong as to be "working on my very bones" (Lucy Mack Smith, *History of Joseph Smith*, p. 139).

Oliver Cowdery had sought and obtained the promise of the Lord that he might act as a translator of the Book of Mormon. Thus it was essential that he be familiar with the spirit of revelation. Preparing Oliver for that experience, the Lord explained, "I will tell you in your mind and in your heart, by the Holy Ghost, which shall come upon you and which shall dwell in your heart." This, the Lord said, "is the spirit of revelation." (D&C 8:2–3.) Oliver started to translate and then faltered. He had not fully recognized the demand on his part to obtain and retain the spirit of revelation. Again, direction was sought to help him understand his inability to receive revelation. "You have not understood," the Lord said; "you have supposed that I would give it unto you, when you took no thought save it was to ask me. But, behold, I say unto you, that you must study it out in your mind; then you must ask me if it be right, and if it is right I will cause that your bosom shall burn within you; therefore, you shall feel that it is right." (D&C 9:7–8.)

The Book of Mormon Opens the Heavens

The Psalmist, looking to a future day, prophesied that "truth shall spring out of the earth; and righteousness shall look down from heaven" (Psalm 85:11). That is, the Book of Mormon shall come forth from the earth, and those accepting its testimony will be blessed with the revelations of heaven. Such, Joseph Smith explained, was an interpretation of the parable of the mustard seed. Be it remembered that Christ likened the kingdom of heaven to a mustard seed, which he said a man sowed in his field, "which indeed is the least of all seeds: but when it is grown, it is the greatest among herbs, and becometh a tree, so that the birds of the air come and lodge in the branches thereof" (Matthew 13:31–32). Commenting on this parable, Joseph Smith said, "Let us take the Book of Mormon, which a man took and hid in his field, securing it by his faith, to spring up in the last days, or in due time; let us behold it coming forth out of the ground, which is indeed accounted the least of all seeds, but behold it branching forth, yea, even towering, with lofty branches, and God-like majesty, until it, like the mustard seed, becomes the greatest of all herbs. And it is truth, and it has sprouted and come forth out of the earth, and righteousness begins to look down from heaven, and God is sending down His powers, gifts and angels, to lodge in the branches thereof." (*Teachings of the Prophet Joseph Smith*, p. 98.)

Acceptance of the Book of Mormon and obtaining the spirit of prophecy and revelation are inseparable. As the Prophet said, the gifts and powers of God lodge in its branches. Brigham Young asserted: "There is not a man or woman that loves truth, who has heard the report of the Book of Mormon, but the Spirit of the Almighty has testified to him or her of its truth" (*Journal of Discourses*, 1:93). We cannot reject the scriptures given to teach the gospel of salvation to our dispensation (the institutional or canonized revelations) and at the same time lay claim to the companionship of the Holy Ghost (the medium of individual revelation). Conversely, we cannot study the canon of scripture without receiving personal revelation, if we are doing so under the influence of the Spirit.

Were we to tell others of the Christian world that it is impossible to reject the Bible—its testimony and teachings—and at the same time have companionship with the Holy Ghost, they would readily agree. If, however, we tell them that it is impossible to reject our testimony of Joseph Smith and the Book of Mormon and have any claim on the spirit of prophecy and revelation, they adamantly disagree (see 2 Nephi 33:10; Mormon 7:8-9). Yet the principle is the same, and the fact that the churches of the Christian world are without the spirit of prophecy and revelation is the evidence. Thus it seems most natural for us to read that the Lord promised those who believe in the doctrines of the Book of Mormon that they would also enjoy the manifestation of his Spirit (D&C 5:16).

The Spirit of Revelation

Describing what it is like to have the spirit of revelation, Joseph Smith said that the "Holy Ghost has no other effect than pure intelligence." It expands the mind, enlightens the understanding, and aids in storing the intellect with knowledge. It is, Joseph said, "calm and serene." "A person may profit," he explained, "by noticing the first intimation of the spirit of revelation; for instance, when you feel pure intelligence flowing into you, it may give you sudden strokes of ideas, so that by noticing it, you may find it fulfilled the same day or soon; (i.e.) those things that were presented unto your minds by the Spirit of God, will come to pass; and thus by learning the Spirit of God and understanding it, you may grow into the principle of revelation, until you become perfect in Christ Jesus." (*Teachings of the Prophet Joseph Smith,* pp. 149–51.)

It takes the same spirit to understand a revelation that it took to obtain it. If purity of heart and faith are essential to call down a revelation from heaven, then purity of heart and faith are equally essential to understanding it. The system by which revelation is dispensed is everlastingly the same. One man will not acquire it "cheaper" than another. If we are going to understand what a prophet understood, we must obtain that understanding as the prophet obtained it.

The Book of Mormon testifies that many plain and precious things have been taken from the Bible, which in turn has caused many to stumble. Why, we are asked, would the Lord allow this to happen? Why would he permit certain truths—truths of salvation —to be withheld from the world? In response, it ought to be observed that the only people who had those truths anciently were those who accepted the prophets and the revelation given for their day; all others were without them. As it was then, so it is now. To accept living prophets is to open the door of salvation and the windows of revelation. Those who refuse to listen to living prophets have also closed the eyes of their understanding to the words of the dead prophets.

At the Last Supper, Christ told the meridian Twelve that he had taught them in proverbs [parables], but that the time would come when he would grant them understanding (John 16:25). He also gave them the promise of another Comforter, even the Holy Ghost, which would teach them all things and bring all things to their remembrance (John 14:26; 16:13–14). But few in Jesus' day understood his message. That understanding came only by the spirit of revelation (see Matthew 16:17). Now, if but few could understand the gospel even as it fell from the lips of the Savior, we are left to wonder how many in our time will understand it as represented in the Bible, which is at best but a small fragment of that which he taught and did. Indeed, the Gospels recount only a few of the events in the life of Jesus of Nazareth; the total number of days identified in the record is little more than a month; and his recorded sayings can be recited in about half an hour. If understanding is to come from the Bible, it must come as it came to those tutored by the Savior himself, and that is by the spirit of revelation. Plainly, without the Holy Ghost there is no meaningful understanding in the realm of spiritual things.

All Are Invited to Stand in the Light

When Joseph Smith parted the clouds of theological darkness that then covered the whole earth, he did so that all who would might stand in heaven's light. "God hath not revealed anything to Joseph," he said, "but what He will make known unto the Twelve, and even the least Saint may know all things as fast as he is able to bear them" (*Teachings of the Prophet Joseph Smith,* p. 149). There is but one plan of salvation, one path to the divine presence. Where prophets have trod, all who will be saved must also tread. To Peter's statement that "no prophecy of the scripture is of any private interpretation" (2 Peter 1:20), we would add that there are no "private doctrines of salvation." As the blessings of the temple are available to all who prepare themselves to enter its sacred portals, so the mysteries of the kingdom of heaven are available to all who have eyes to see and ears to hear.

The companionship of the Holy Ghost, or the spirit of inspiration and revelation, is not confined to those holding either tenure or position in the kingdom of God. As Elder Bruce R. McConkie observed: "The visions of eternity are not reserved for Apostles—they are not reserved for the General Authorities. Revelation is something that should be received by every individual. God is no respecter of persons, and every soul, in the ultimate sense, is just as precious in his sight as the souls of those who are called to positions of leadership." Because God operates on "principles of eternal, universal, and never-deviating law," anyone who abides the law that entitles him to get revelation can know exactly what the President of the Church knows, "can entertain angels just as well as Joseph Smith entertained them, and can be in tune in full measure with all of the things of the Spirit." ("How to Get Personal Revelation," pp. 46, 48.)

It is fundamental to the gospel plan that every accountable soul have both the capacity and the opportunity to know the verities of salvation by personal revelation. Indeed, there can be no impersonal revelations where salvation is concerned. All things are to be known either by manifestation or by confirmation of the Spirit. Teaching this principle, Joseph Smith observed: "Reading the experience of others, or the revelation given to *them*, can never give *us* a comprehensive view of our condition and true relation to God. Knowledge of these things can only be obtained by experience through the ordinances of God set forth for that purpose. Could you gaze into heaven five minutes, you would know more than you would by reading all that ever was written on the subject." (*Teachings of the Prophet Joseph Smith*, p. 324.)

We must know the truths of salvation for ourselves. As we must stand alone on the day of judgment, so our knowledge of gospel truths must stand independent.

Criticism of Modern Revelation

Criticism of modern revelation is born of ignorance as to how revelation comes. Plainly stated, the critics of Joseph Smith and the Book of Mormon wouldn't know a revelation if they saw one. For that matter, the people of the Bible-believing world who accept only that book as scripture cannot even agree among themselves as to what belongs in the Bible and what does not. Luther had little use for the Gospels, and even less for the books of Hebrews, James, Jude, and Revelation, which he would just as soon have excluded from the canon of scripture (E. J. Goodspeed, *How Came the Bible?* p. 89). He also found it necessary, in his German-language Bible, to add the word *alone* to a statement of Paul

(Romans 3:8) so that the ancient prophet could be cited as an authority for the doctrine that salvation is by grace *alone* (R. L. Anderson, *Understanding Paul,* p. 178). Eusebius of Caesarea, known as the father of church history, writing early in the fourth century, divided the books vying for a place in the canon into three categories—acknowledged writings, disputed, and spurious. Jude, James, 2 Peter, and 2 and 3 John were generally considered to be "disputed" books, while many considered the Apocalypse of John, or book of Revelation, to be "spurious." (Eusebius, *Ecclesiastical History,* iii.25.1–4, p. 87.) Joseph Smith held the Song of Solomon to be an uninspired writing (R. J. Matthews, "*A Plainer Translation,*" p. 87), while the famed Rabbi Akiba said that if scripture was holy, the Song of Solomon was the holy of holies (R. K. Harrison, *Introduction to the Old Testament,* p. 1051).

Not only is the world unable to agree upon what ought to be regarded as scripture, but they are equally unable to agree upon its interpretation, and they have thus divided themselves into virtually countless denominations. Nor does this matter of scriptural abuse end here. Historically, Bible tests to discern prophets have consistently been used to reject prophets, and scriptural arguments have been consistently used to reject scripture. From it all we conclude that no test of discernment can rise above the integrity and wisdom of those using it. As to our testimony of the Prophet Joseph Smith, we are quite satisfied to let him speak for himself, which he did in the following language:

> By the power of God I translated the Book of Mormon from hieroglyphics, the knowledge of which was lost to the world, in which wonderful event I stood alone, an unlearned youth, to combat the worldly wisdom and multiplied ignorance of eighteen centuries, with a new revelation, which (if they would receive the everlasting Gospel), would open the eyes of more than eight hundred millions of people, and make "plain the old paths," wherein if a man walk in all the ordinances of God blameless, he shall inherit eternal life; and Jesus Christ, who was, and is, and is to come, has borne me safely over every snare and plan laid in secret or openly, through priestly hypocrisy, sectarian prejudice, popular phi-

losophy, executive power, or law-defying mobocracy, to destroy me.

If, then, the hand of God in all these things that I have accomplished towards the salvation of a priest-ridden generation, in the short space of twelve years, through the boldness of the plan of preaching the Gospel, and the boldness of the means of declaring repentance and baptism for the remission of sins, and a reception of the Holy Ghost by laying on of the hands, agreeable to the authority of the Priesthood, and the still more bold measures of receiving direct revelation from God, through the Comforter, as promised, and by which means all holy men from ancient times till now have spoken and revealed the will of God to men, with the consequent "success" of the gathering of the Saints, throws any "charm" around my being, and "points me out as the most extraordinary man of the age," it demonstrates the fact that truth is mighty and must prevail, and that one man empowered from Jehovah has more influence with the children of the kingdom than eight hundred millions led by the precepts of men. God exalts the humble, and debases the haughty. (*History of the Church*, 6:74.)

Conclusion

Faithful acceptance of the prophets and revelations of one's own dispensation, more specifically of one's own day, is the key to obtaining personal revelation. It would be counterproductive for God to respond to people's personal requests for revealed understanding if those people are not willing to accept for their direction and salvation those the Lord has chosen as his spokesmen and the revelations that come through them. Were God to grant revelation to those who had ignored or denounced the testimony of his anointed servants, he would thereby reward the obstinate and rebellious, making them all the more independent of the discipline of true discipleship.

Those who were contemporary with Christ, who heard and rejected his profession of divine sonship, can hardly make credible claim to the spirit of revelation. So it is with any who reject the servants who have come in the name of the Master. On the other hand, those who accepted Christ or those who accepted the messengers he sent in his stead have always been blessed with the power to open the heavens and obtain personal revelation.

3

Counterfeit Spirits

Verily I say unto you, that there are many spirits which are false spirits, which have gone forth in the earth, deceiving the world. And also Satan hath sought to deceive you, that he might overthrow you.
—*D&C 50:2–3*

As shadows are cast by the shining of light, so are the dark forms of delusive spirits the inseparable companions of all heaven-sent truths. Joseph Smith declared that whenever God has set up his kingdom on the earth the devil has always placed his kingdom there in opposition (*Teachings of the Prophet Joseph Smith*, p. 365). When the kingdom of God is on the earth, Jedediah M. Grant explained, you may expect to see a special display or manifestation of that gospel, priesthood, and kingdom that stands opposed to the light of heaven (*Journal of Discourses*, 2:11). Orson Pratt attested that "our world is infested with those spirits of darkness which were, in the beginning, cast down from the Almighty, in consequence of their rebellion against Him; and in every age of the world these wicked spirits have manifested themselves, and especially when the Priesthood has been upon the earth and a dispensation has been committed from Heaven to man; then all hell has seemed to be in an uproar, and the power of all the fallen angels made manifest" (*Journal of Discourses*, 13:62).

The Opposition of Devils

Reference to the Sacred Grove immediately recalls to our minds that hallowed moment when the Father and the Son appeared to the youthful Joseph Smith and opened this, the greatest of all gospel dispensations. Yet it ought also be remembered that this sacred spot was the place where the prince of darkness opened his counterdispensation as he sought Joseph's destruction. The Prophet would later observe that "the adversary was aware, at a very early period of my life, that I was destined to prove a disturber and an annoyer of his kingdom" (Joseph Smith—History 1:20).

Perhaps it was to be expected that the first miracle in the newly organized Church would be the casting out of a devil. This took place in Colesville, Broome County, New York, when Joseph Smith, acting in the name of Christ, cast a devil out of Newel Knight, who was thrown about while terrified neighbors and relatives looked on (*History of the Church*, 1:82–83). The prince of darkness found greater success, however, by confusing the Saints with revelations of his own making. Memorable examples include Hiram Page and his "peepstone" by which he obtained revelations concerning the upbuilding of Zion and the organization of the Church—which revelations were very much at odds with those received by the Prophet (see D&C 28)—and also a woman by the name of Hubble, who professed to be a prophetess and who also revealed commandments and laws for the supposed benefit of the Church (D&C 43).

Along with these spurious revelations, the Church witnessed a veritable parade of counterfeit spiritual experiences. Thus the Prophet was warned that "there are many spirits which are false spirits, which have gone forth in the earth, deceiving the world." He was told that these spirits sought his overthrow along with the destruction of the Church. Nevertheless, the Lord affirmed that all true doctrine and all genuine testimony must be rooted in revelation or it "is not of God." Thus Joseph learned that it was not enough to have scripture, for devils carry Bibles; rather one must have the scriptures and the spirit of revelation, meaning the companionship of the Holy Ghost. Without the Holy Ghost, that which was said and done could not be acceptable to God and would of necessity "be rooted up" (D&C 50:1–3, 14–20; Matthew 15:13).

This left but two ploys to the father of all lies in his war with revealed truth: to relentlessly oppose the principle of revelation and deny the power of godliness or to proliferate all manner of counterfeit revelations to keep the Saints constantly confused. The great rebel of heaven chose to divide his forces and attack from both flanks. Thus, while priestcraft led the assault against the principle of revelation, the infant Church was deluged with counterfeit spirits. Describing this storm of deception, Joseph Smith wrote:

> Soon after the Gospel was established in Kirtland, and during the absence of the authorities of the Church, many false spirits were introduced, many strange visions were seen, and wild, enthusiastic notions were entertained; men ran out of doors under the influence of this spirit, and some of them got upon the stumps of trees and shouted, and all kinds of extravagances were entered into by them; one man pursued a ball that he said he saw flying in the air, until he came to a precipice, when he jumped into the top of a tree, which saved his life; and many ridiculous things were entered into, *calculated to bring disgrace upon the Church of God, to cause the Spirit of God to be withdrawn, and to uproot and destroy those glorious principles which had been developed for the salvation of the human family.* But when the authorities returned, the spirit was made manifest, those members that were exercised with it were tried for their fellowship, and those that would not repent and forsake it were cut off. (*Teachings of the Prophet Joseph Smith,* pp. 213–14, italics added.)

Of particular moment in the Prophet's statement is the observation that these counterfeit spirits are an offense to the true Spirit of the Lord, causing it to withdraw, and that their purpose and design are to destroy confidence in the spirit of revelation, and of course to bring the Church into disrepute. Describing these same events Elder Parley P. Pratt said: "As I went forth among the different branches, some very strange spiritual operations were manifested, which were disgusting, rather than edifying. Some persons would seem to swoon away, and make unseemly gestures, and be drawn or disfigured in their countenances. Others would fall into ecstasies, and be drawn into contortions, cramps, fits, etc. Others would seem to have visions and revelations, which were not edifying, and which were not congenial to the doctrine and spirit of the gospel. In short, a false and lying spirit seemed to be creeping into the Church." (*Autobiography of Parley P. Pratt,* p. 61.)

These events remind us of the experience of the Apostle Paul. A young woman possessed with a spirit of divination followed him and his companions around, testifying that they were "servants of the most high God" and that they would show the people "the way of salvation." After some time, Paul came to the realization that even though her testimony was true it was of the wrong source, whereupon he cast a devil out of her. (Acts 16:16–18.) Why, it ought be asked, would an evil spirit testify in such a manner? Indeed, its doing so was most clever. To this damsel possessed with a devil it would give credence among the members of the Church, placing her in a position to do much evil. Because soothsaying, which the young woman did, was strictly forbidden by the law of Moses, it would close Jewish doors to the missionaries' proselyting efforts among them. Finally, it would convey the idea to the Gentiles that Christianity did not differ in principle or power from their own systems of worship.

There are two courses of action that make people particularly susceptible to delusive spirits: willful disobedience and, conversely, excessive zeal in keeping the commandments. Strangely enough, the latter is as dangerous as the first, if not more so. Let us give brief consideration to each.

Transgression Opens the Door to False Revelation

In a revelation calling missionaries to labor with the Shakers (United Society of Believers in Christ's Second Appearing), a sect among whom supernatural experiences were claimed, as witnessed by their name, the Lord said: "They desire to know the truth in part, but not all, for they are not right before me and must needs repent" (D&C 49:2). This is an apt and succinct description of many who have been enticed by false spirits and "received them to be of God" (D&C 50:15). Through transgression and ignorance many have been "seduced by evil spirits, or doctrines of devils, or the commandments of men" (D&C 46:7).

   "Sin-laden souls are easily led from the truth," wrote Elder Bruce R. McConkie. "In their carnal state they find it easier to believe their sins are removed simply by confessing the Lord Jesus with their lips, or through the performance of some act of penitence, rather than by following the hard and rugged course of seeking repentance in tears and anguish." (*Doctrinal New Testament Commentary*, 3:111.) Paul, for instance, wrote of those who "creep unto houses, and lead captive silly women laden with sins, led away with divers lusts," and added that such would be "ever learning, and never able to come to the knowledge of the truth" (2 Timothy 3:6-7). Spiritual truths elude them because they have polluted the tabernacle of their souls and the Spirit cannot reside therein.

   Commenting on the claims of members of the Church to having been the recipients of great spiritual manifestations, Brigham Young said:

   I say to such persons, Go ahead, and get all the revelations you can. If brother Joseph visits you every night, go ahead, and tell him to bring brother Hyrum, father Smith, Don Carlos Smith, St. Paul, Peter, James, and John, and Jesus Christ, if you can induce him to do so. But I could almost lay my hand on that Bible and swear that the man or woman who gets such revelations has been guilty of adultery, or of theft, or has been rebellious and apostatized in feelings, but has come back again, and now professes to have such revelations. Hell is full of such revelations; and I could almost testify that a man or woman who receives them has been guilty of some outrageous crime. I have had men come to me and tell the wonderful great dreams and visions which they have, when those very persons have apostatized heretofore, have denied their God and their religion; and I knew it. Many come to me and tell me what wonderful visions they have—that their minds are open to eternal things—

that they can see visions of eternity open before them and
understand all about this kingdom, — many of whom have at
some time been guilty of betraying their brethren, or committing some atrocious crime. I never notice them much. I sit
and hear them talk about their wonderful knowledge, but it
passes in and out of my ears like the sound of the wind. It is
for me to see to this kingdom, that it is built up, and to pre-
serve the Saints from the grasp of the enemy. The visions of
the class I have mentioned are nothing to me. They may ex-
hibit their great knowledge before me; but when they have
done, it is all gone from me. (*Journal of Discourses,* 5:352.)

Spiritual Excesses Lead to False Revelations

Any virtue overdone becomes a vice. This is as true of spiritual
things as it is of temporal things. Christ explicitly commanded that
we are neither to add to nor to take from the law of the gospel.
"Whoso shall declare more or less than this," he warned, "and establish it for my doctrine, the same cometh of evil, and is not built
upon my rock; but he buildeth upon a sandy foundation, and the
gates of hell stand open to receive such when the floods come and
the winds beat upon them" (3 Nephi 11:40). Thus, those who become truer than true, who become super zealots taking pride in the
way they live the commandments, become susceptible to false revelations and counterfeit manifestations.

"I do not like to see men and women that want to be a little
ahead of anybody else — a little ahead of the Prophets of God," observed Patriarch John Young.

> The Spirit of the Lord is liberally enjoyed by the Saints
> generally; and if they continue, they will hold converse with
> the servants of God who are behind the veil. But that time is
> not yet.
>
> Some of the brethren and sisters tell of their receiving
> visits from Joseph, Hyrum, brother Grant, and others. Such
> persons must look out for their ship; for, if they do not
> watch, just as sure as you are born, they will run under and

be overcome. When a man or woman comes and tells me that he or she is visited by the Prophets and Apostles that are gone beyond the veil, and that they have these communications day and night, and all the time, – that they have the opportunity of conversing with the spirits of just men made perfect, – I will just say that the Devil is in them, and not the Lord. I wonder if the Lord loves them so much better than the Prophets that he would send to them all the heavenly hosts? (*Journal of Discourses*, 5:373.)

Paul spoke of zeal without knowledge in reference to those Jews who prided themselves in keeping the law, and yet who ignorantly rejected the Messiah. "Being ignorant of God's righteousness," he said, "and going about to establish their own righteousness," they failed to understand that "Christ is the end of the law" (Romans 10:1-4). As the Pharisees' pride in the magnificence of their observance of ritual and law blinded them to its purpose, so do their modern counterparts lose their spiritual balance as they become infatuated with their own holiness. These become ready prey for clever devils waiting to manifest all the mysteries of heaven to them. "We would do well to have a sane, rounded, and balanced approach to the whole gospel and all of its doctrines," Elder Bruce R. McConkie observed. When we get fanatical in one area, it is a short step to fanaticism in another. "All of the doctrines and practices of the Church are taught publicly. There are no secret doctrines, no private practices, no courses of conduct approved for a few only. The blessings of the gospel are for all men. Do not be deceived into believing that the General Authorities believe any secret doctrines or have any private ways of living. Everything that is taught and practiced in the Church is open to public inspection, or at least, where temple ordinances are concerned, to the inspection and knowledge of everyone who qualifies himself by personal righteousness to enter the house of the Lord." ("To Honest Truth Seekers," pp. 4-5.)

William E. Berrett wisely observed that "those who pray that the Spirit might give them immediate guidance in every little thing throw themselves open to false spirits that seem ever ready to answer our pleas and confuse us. . . . The people I have found most confused in this Church are those who seek personal revelations on everything. They want the personal assurance from the Spirit from daylight to dark on everything they do. I say they are the most confused people I know because it appears sometimes that the answer comes from the wrong source."

Illustrating the principle, Brother Berrett told a story of a couple of missionaries in the woods of Arkansas.

They saw some large, razor-backed hogs which were just as thin as rails, but they were never still a moment. They would rush off to this edge of the clearing and stick their noses up in the air as if they were listening and then back over there and stick their noses up in the air. They were going every minute and were just as thin as shadows. The missionaries looked at them and were a little surprised. Off to the side of the clearing there was a log cabin, and out in front was an old man sitting whittling. The missionaries were curious enough to go over and talk to him.

They said, "It's pretty nice country you have here."

"It is for those who like it."

"Have you lived here all your life?"

"Not yet."

They said, "Say, can you tell us what's wrong with those hogs over there? They just run and dart around hither and yonder and act as if they were listening, and back again as if they were listening."

"Well," he said in a hoarse, barely discernible voice, "I'll tell ya how it was. Those are my hogs. I was getting them ready for market, so I was giving them corn. They would come for the corn when they heard me call. Then I got this cold and I couldn't call them any more; so I went out and rapped on the pan, and now I'm in a real fix. The woodpeckers are running them to death."

I have seen woodpeckers running people to death, and they think it is a matter of revelation—listening constantly, you see, for this warning of the Spirit, not differentiating that which comes from God and that which comes too often from the wrong source, so that people are left in confusion." ("Teaching by the Spirit," pp. 102–3.)

The very purposes of mortality would be frustrated were it possible for us to receive revelation on all things. Indeed, the canon of scripture warns against the danger of excessive dependence upon the powers of heaven to assure our salvation. "It is not meet that I should command in all things," the Lord declared, "for he that is compelled in all things, the same is a slothful and not a wise servant; wherefore he receiveth no reward." Surely he is an unwise servant who, having been taught correct principles, cannot then use those principles to govern himself. The power is in us, the revelation affirms, wherein we are agents unto ourselves. "And inasmuch as men do good they shall in nowise lose their reward." But by way of warning the Almighty stated: "He that doeth not anything until he is commanded, and receiveth a commandment with doubtful heart, and keepeth it with slothfulness, the same is damned." (D&C 58:26–29.)

"A man [meaning a righteous and good person] may receive the Holy Ghost, and it may descend upon him and not tarry with him" (D&C 130:23). In harmony with such a declaration, Elder Boyd K. Packer said, "I have learned that strong, impressive spiritual experiences do not come to us very frequently." Further, he observed that "it is not wise to wrestle with the revelations with such insistence as to demand immediate answers or blessings to your liking. You cannot force spiritual things. Such words as *compel, coerce, constrain, pressure, demand* do not describe our privileges with the Spirit. You can no more force the Spirit to respond than you can force a bean to sprout, or an egg to hatch before its time. You can create a climate to foster growth; you can nourish, and protect; but you cannot force or compel: You must await the growth." (*"That All May Be Edified,"* pp. 337–38.)

There are great dangers associated with those who profess a constant outpouring of the spirit of revelation. Frequently, those so professing place themselves above the need to listen to the counsel and direction of their priesthood leaders. Often they are above correction. It is natural for those who suppose they are having regular conversations with angels and diverse exalted beings to be a little bemused at the counsel of bishops and stake presidents. With but a bit of polish, such an attitude ripens into the cultist's mentality in which one is above the laws of both church and state. Such persons know no discipline save that which has been revealed to them, and then only to impose it on others. Their revelations become a cover for all the sins they have committed and the justification for those they will yet commit.

To What Extent Can Satan Deceive Us?

Frequently the question is asked, To what extent can Satan deceive us? Generally the answer is, Only to the extent that we allow him to do so. We open the door to his beguilements through disobedience or by rejecting heaven-sent truths when we know them to be such. Any course of action that is offensive to the Spirit of the Lord is attractive to the spirit of adversary. To offend the one is to invite the other. Paul illustrated the principle when he said that God would send a "strong delusion" to those who had "pleasure in unrighteousness" (2 Thessalonians 2:11–12). Jacob applied the principle to those of exaggerated religious zeal. From these God took the plainness of his gospel and gave them things in its place that they could not understand. "Because they desired it," Jacob said, "God hath done it, that they may stumble" (Jacob 4:14).

"We should be on guard always to resist Satan's advances," wrote President Joseph Fielding Smith. "He will appear to us in the person of a friend or a relative in whom we have confidence. He has power to place thoughts in our minds and to whisper to us in unspoken impressions to entice us to satisfy our appetites or desires and in various other ways he plays upon our weaknesses and desires." (*Answers to Gospel Questions*, 3:81.) Satan can and will appear as an angel of light. By revelation we have been given the keys by which the true and false messengers can be detected (D&C 129).

The earth is full of false Christs and false prophets—false systems of salvation, false doctrine, and false notions of that which the prophets are and have written—such that "if possible, they shall deceive the very elect . . . according to the covenant." And yet the Lord has promised that "whoso treasureth up my word, shall not be deceived." (Joseph Smith—Matthew 1:22, 37.) Those whose loins are "girt about with truth," who are wearing the "breastplate of righteousness," and whose feet are "shod with the preparation of the gospel" will be preserved (D&C 27:16).

Conclusion

Since the days of Adam, the earth has not known an era in which there has been a greater outpouring of eternal truths from the heavens than in this, the dispensation of the fulness of times. Our dispensation was initiated by the appearance of the Father and the Son and was followed shortly by the appearance of the prophets who have stood at the head of every dispensation in ages past, each "declaring their dispensation, their rights, their keys, their honors, their majesty and glory, and the power of their priesthood" (D&C 128:21). Every spiritual gift and power known to the ancients has been or will be restored to us. Not the least of these spiritual powers is the companionship of the Holy Ghost, which is granted to every faithful Saint as he or she lays claim to membership in the Church through the ordinance of baptism.

We hardly expect such an outpouring of light to go unnoticed or unanswered by the prince of darkness; it has ever been the case that each dispensation is met by a counterdispensation. Those devils not deployed in the denial of the principle of revelation are employed in counterfeiting it. Those most susceptible to the evil spirits' wiles are the disobedient and the super-zealous—those who have laid aside their armor and those attempting to wear a coat of mail and carry a sword far too heavy for them. Thus the restored kingdom is constantly under siege, as it were, by those denying the existence of angels and those seeing angels where there are none. "Nothing," said Joseph Smith, "is a greater injury to the children of men than to be under the influence of a false spirit when they think they have the Spirit of God" (*Teachings of the Prophet Joseph Smith,* p. 205). Our protection simply rests in knowing and living the gospel.

4

Try the Spirits

Put your trust in that Spirit which leadeth to do good—yea, to do justly, to walk humbly, to judge righteously; and this is my Spirit.

—D&C 11:12

Members of the Church do not have the right to be without the spirit of revelation. In scriptural writ we are "commanded" to inquire of God "in all things" and are assured that he will respond "liberally." Having done so we are obligated to do as the "Spirit testifies," and to do so "in all holiness of heart, walking uprightly" before God, considering the end of our salvation. Our spirit is to be one of prayer and of thanksgiving in order that we not "be seduced by evil spirits, or doctrines of devils, or the commandments of men; for some are of men, and others of devils." (D&C 46:7.)

The God of heaven has chosen "the weak and the simple" to carry the message of salvation to the ends of the earth (D&C 1:23). This assures that the message will not be confused with the messenger. By contrast, the prince of darkness prefers the clever and the articulate to be his ambassadors. The untrained and unlettered can declare truth, while sophistication and erudition often characterize a message which is false. Given that both men and devils so frequently imitate the form of godliness, it is absolutely necessary that the Saints have the spirit of discernment. To that end let us review seven basic principles by which we are to "try the spirits."

What Purpose Is Being Served?

One of the most direct and effective tests of discernment is to simply ask the question, What is the purpose of this professed manifestation or religious experience? Every missionary, for instance, has met scores of people who rejected them and their message obstinately because they "have already been saved," because they have had some kind of a supernatural experience, or because they have made some sort of a verbal confession; they are thereby excused from the responsibility or need to hear the message of the Restoration. The experience is so common and sometimes the people seem so sincere that the missionaries are left to wonder if, in at least some instances, there is not some legitimacy to the claim.

When we measure such professions by the question, What is their purpose? they are found woefully wanting. What is taking place in our example is that someone is essentially saying to the missionaries, "God gave me a spiritual experience, or I have made a confession of faith, and therefore I have no need for the ordinances of baptism for the remission of sins. My sins don't need to be remitted, nor am I in need of the companionship or gift of the Holy Ghost. Furthermore, I have no need for the counsel of living prophets, the blessings and authority of the priesthood, or such things as the temple endowment and eternal marriage. My spiritual experience makes me independent of all such things." And thus they close the door to citizenship in the church and kingdom of God and to the opportunity to receive the fulness of gospel blessings.

No special spiritual insight is necessary to see the complete inconsistency of such a profession. It closes the door to every privilege and blessing associated with citizenship in God's kingdom, and, conveniently enough, it closes the door to every obligation and sacrifice also associated with such citizenship. In contrast to this, almost countless stories can be told by faithful Latter-day Saints of how they or some other member of their family had some kind of special spiritual experience that prepared them to accept the gospel message. The difference between the genuine and the counterfeit spiritual experience is that one opens the door to blessings and obligations while the other closes that same door to both.

"That which doth not edify," the scriptures declare, "is not of God, and is darkness" (D&C 50:23). To edify is to build or to improve, to open to our view the light of heaven. That which edifies opens the doors of faith, repentance, and baptism. It opens the doors of commitment and sacrifice, requires a broken heart and a contrite spirit, and closes the doors of darkness and sin. That which edifies neither is self-serving nor does it allow for self-justification, both of which are characteristics common to counterfeit revelations.

Channels

"It is contrary to the economy of God," declared Joseph Smith, "for any member of the Church, or any one, to receive instruction for those in authority, higher than themselves" (*Teachings of the Prophet Joseph Smith,* p. 21). It would be a mistake for anyone to give heed to such a manifestation. "Should you receive a vision or revelation from the Almighty," Brigham Young explained, "one that the Lord gave you concerning yourselves, or this people, but which you are not to reveal on account of your not being the proper person, or because it ought not to be known by the people at present, you should shut it up and seal it as close, and lock it as tight as heaven is to you, and make it as secret as the grave." Then he added: "The Lord has no confidence in those who reveal secrets, for He cannot safely reveal Himself to such persons." (*Journal of Discourses,* 4:288.)

The man who stands at the head of the church and kingdom of God is the covenant spokesman. We sustain him as a prophet, seer, and revelator. "His word," the Lord said, "ye shall receive, as if from mine own mouth, in all patience and faith." When we do so we have the promise that the "gates of hell" will not prevail against us and that "the Lord God will disperse the powers of darkness" from before us and "cause the heavens to shake" for our good "and his name's glory." (D&C 21:5–6.) Paradoxically, if we attend to the channels the Lord has ordained, even should they be in error on some point, we will be blessed, while those who choose instead to heed other voices lose themselves in a maze of darkness. Those who ignore the holy order of God to chase revelations do not receive them, while those who trust the Lord's spokesmen are blessed with the knowledge of a sure course ("the gates of hell shall not prevail against" them) and are further rewarded with the spirit of revelation as the "powers of darkness" are dispersed before them.

As the prophet is the Lord's spokesman to the Church, so a stake president is the covenant spokesman to his stake, a bishop to his ward, a quorum president to his quorum, and a father to his family. This does not suggest a doctrine of infallibility on the part of priesthood leaders any more than it suggests that all fathers are infallible. It is, however, a declaration that we have a divine obligation to sustain those whom God has chosen to stand at the head and be his spokesmen. It is understood by every Latter-day Saint that we no more sustain a man in unrighteousness than we would sustain the devil himself.

An interesting illustration of the unequivocal nature of the principle that only one man can receive revelation for the Church and that no one can receive revelation for anyone in authority higher than himself is the temporary provision that existed in the government of the Church to select a successor to Joseph Smith, should that have been necessary before the organization of the Quorum of the Twelve. Though the Church was organized in April of 1830, the first Apostles were not called until February of 1835. Thus, in case Joseph should prove unworthy of his position at the helm of the Church, the Lord instructed the Saints that in those circumstances he would "not have power" except to appoint his successor (see D&C 43:4). Since Joseph Smith was called of God, if he lost favor with God, God would have to release him. Since God had established the provision that none but the man standing at the head can receive revelation for the Church, God would still give through his wayward prophet the revelation to correct the situation. It might be observed that if that had happened it would not have been the first time a prophet was voice to a revelation that was contrary to his own will.

The Lord simply will not violate the channels that he has chosen. For him to do so, even in a single instance, would be to introduce an endless array of confusion into all the affairs of his king-

dom—no longer would the Lord's house be "a house of order."
Only one man at a time can stand at the helm of the good ship Zion,
and no sailor, regardless of how well intentioned he may be, has
the right to relieve his commanding officer and change the course
and destiny of the ship because he feels "moved" to do so.

Nor is it in the purview of the membership of the Church to add
to or take from the canon of scripture, either of which is a denial
of the spirit of the Holy Ghost. It is not for the membership of the
Church to add to or edit scriptural writ, which in spirit is what happens when we read with a blind eye or a practiced selectivity, refusing to see what we do not want to see or claiming to see that
which is not there.

Obedience: The Grand Key

Because of delusive spirits that troubled the youthful Church,
the Lord gave Joseph Smith "a pattern in all things" in order that
he and the membership of the Church not be deceived. That revelation reads as follows:

> Wherefore he that prayeth, whose spirit is contrite, the
> same is accepted of me if he obey mine ordinances.
>
> He that speaketh, whose spirit is contrite, whose language
> is meek and edifieth, the same is of God if he obey mine or-
> dinances.
>
> And again, he that trembleth under my power shall be
> made strong, and shall bring forth fruits of praise and wis-
> dom, according to the revelations and truths which I have
> given you.
>
> And again, he that is overcome and bringeth not forth
> fruits, even according to this pattern, is not of me.
>
> Wherefore, by this pattern ye shall know the spirits in all
> cases under the whole heavens. (D&C 52:15–19.)

This divine standard for the discerning of spirits ought to be
carefully studied. It begins with the announcement that the prayer
of the contrite is acceptable *if* they are obedient to the ordinances.
The word *contrite* "first meant rubbed together, bruised, crushed;
but then was applied to those crushed by their sense of sin, there-

fore repentant'' (Joseph T. Shipley, *Dictionary of Word Origins*, p. 355). The word *ordinance* does not refer primarily to rites or rituals, but rather has a broader reach which embraces all the laws and statutes of the Lord. Thus the thrust of the above verses is that the prayer of the genuinely repentant is acceptable to God if they have embraced the law of the gospel and have commenced living it. So it is in regard to all professed manifestations of the Spirit; a viable test of legitimacy is conformity to the order of the kingdom of God.

The standard is the same for those who speak, preach, or teach the gospel. Their efforts are acceptable only to the extent that they too are contrite of spirit and seek to live the principles that they are attempting to teach. There can be no hypocrisy here. It is further expected that their language will be meek—not meaning that it lacks boldness or assurance, but rather that it is not overbearing or contentious—and that what they teach edifies, meaning that it encourages and builds rather than condemns and assaults.

We are then told that those who have embraced a true spirit will be "made strong," or, in the language of another revelation, their "confidence [will] wax strong in the presence of God" (D&C 121:45). Having a testimony born of the Spirit, they will have a sense of spiritual independence and will not find it necessary to lean upon others for their spiritual support. Their lives will be rich in the fruits of the gospel, including a spirit of thanksgiving and wisdom unknown to the carnally minded. We are also assured that their lives and what they teach will be in harmony with the revelations and truths already granted the Saints.

Any who are overcome by the power of a spirit that does not have these characteristics (true humility, a spirit of repentance, meekness of language, goodness of doctrine, and general gospel obedience, i.e., a purity of life and purpose), we are told, are not of God. Such, we are assured, is the pattern "in all cases under the whole heavens."

Subjection to the Prophets

All who have been given the gift of the Holy Ghost are entitled to the spirit of prophecy and the spirit of revelation. Thus we have no professional ministry but rather are called upon to instruct one another that "all may be edified of all" (D&C 88:122). Paul taught this principle to the Corinthian Saints, saying, "ye may all prophesy one by one, that all may learn, and all may be comforted." He also established proper boundaries for such expressions, saying, "the spirits of the prophets are subject to the prophets. For God is not the author of confusion, but of peace, as in all churches of the saints." (1 Corinthians 14:31–33.) This is simply to say that the spirit of prophecy will not be found at odds with the testimony and teachings of the prophets whose words are recorded in the scriptures, nor will they be at odds with the declarations of our living oracles. Truth cannot be at odds with itself.

A Fit Tabernacle

"Know ye not that ye are the temple of God, and that the Spirit of God dwelleth in you?" Paul asked of the Corinthian Saints. This scripture frequently is interpreted as referring to one's physical body as a temple, but it has a wider meaning also. Paul was indicating that in former times the whole congregation of Israel was considered to be the "temple" or habitation of God, because He dwelt among them. Thus Paul likened the Saints at Corinth to the temple of God because they had the same entitlement to the divine presence as their ancient counterparts. The Apostle then added the warning that "if any man defile the temple of God [that is, teach false doctrine or introduce improper practices into the Church], "him shall God destroy; for the temple of God is holy, which temple ye are." (1 Corinthians 3:16–17.) As this principle is true of the congregation of the Saints, so it is true of each member individually. Speaking of personal sins, Paul inquired again: "Know ye not that your body is the temple of the Holy Ghost which is in you, which ye have of God, and ye are not your own? For ye are bought with a price: therefore glorify God in your body, and in your spirit, which are God's." (1 Corinthians 6:19–20.) Again the message is that neither God nor his Spirit will dwell in an unclean tabernacle. The pure waters of everlasting life cannot pour forth from an impure vessel.

Purity is prerequisite for the spirit of revelation. The baptism of water precedes the baptism of the Spirit. "The wisdom that is from above," James wrote, "is first pure, then peaceable, gentle, and easy to be intreated, full of mercy and good fruits, without partiality, and without hypocrisy" (James 3:17). "The word of God is a manifestation of the nature and character of God. As God cannot lack wisdom, so the revelations of heaven cannot be unwise; as God cannot lack virtue, purity, or any other godly attribute, so the revelations of heaven cannot lack these attributes. The spirit of revelation affects the heart and soul of man, not only creating an abhorrence for sin, but also giving birth to a 'disposition . . . to do good continually.' (Mosiah 5:2; Alma 13:12.)" (Joseph Fielding McConkie, *Prophets and Prophecy,* p. 166.)

To those questioning the revelations given to Joseph Smith, the Lord said, "Ye know that there is no unrighteousness in them, and that which is righteous cometh down from above, from the Father of lights" (D&C 67:9). Further, the Lord promised that "if ye are purified and cleansed from all sin, ye shall ask whatsoever you will in the name of Jesus and it shall be done. But know this, it shall be given you what you shall ask" (D&C 50:29–30; see also 3 Nephi 8:1). Those who receive the promise from the Lord that whatever they ask will be given are those who have proven to the Lord that they will not ask for that which they should not (see Helaman 10:5).

Divine Truth Is Always Subject to Confirmation

"If you behold a spirit manifested that you cannot understand," the Lord told Joseph Smith, "and you receive not that spirit, ye shall ask of the Father in the name of Jesus; and if he give not unto you that spirit, then you may know that it is not of God" (D&C 50:31). That which is of God is subject to confirmation. There is no danger of exhausting the light of heaven—it need not be rationed. It is not as if we were limited to one spiritual manifestation that Joseph Smith is a prophet or that Jesus is the Christ. Such witnesses or confirmations are constant, and as it is the case with the testimony of Joseph Smith and Jesus Christ, so it is with all the truths of heaven. Constancy in living a principle assures a constant harvest of its fruits.

Our testimony of Christ must be more than an echo from the hills of Palestine and Judea. While we savor the memory of exceptional spiritual experiences and associations, it requires more than that to sustain a healthy and vibrant spirit. As we seek to advance in understanding, we will be confronted by unfamiliar spirits. Such spirits are easily discerned if they find no harmony with other principles of truth and if they are not readily affirmed by that God from whence they claim to have come.

That Which Provokes the Adversary

There is no middle ground where the doctrines of salvation are concerned. As the rays of the morning sun are incompatible with the darkness of night, so the revelations of heaven are a discordant sound to the minions of hell. A doctrine they do not oppose is not worth notice; a spirit that does not offend them is not celestial in nature. A sure test of all good doctrine is to ask who likes it and who does not. Similarly, a spirit that does not provoke the wrath of the adversary is not the Lord's Spirit. (See Joseph Fielding McConkie and Robert L. Millet, *Sustaining and Defending the Faith*, chapter 1.)

Conclusion

If the ability to discern spirits were not within the grasp of the humblest of Saints, surely a just God could not hold them accountable should they be deceived. As all men are expected to recognize, accept, and live the principles of the gospel, so they are expected to discern the evil one—even when he appears as an angel of light. That we make mistakes as we grow to spiritual maturity is not a matter of any particular moment. What is important is that we live so that we are fit company for the Holy Ghost and that we are not ignorant of the principles by which spirits are discerned.

5

Spiritual Instincts

And the Spirit giveth light to every man that cometh into the world; and the Spirit enlighteneth every man through the world, that hearkeneth to the voice of the Spirit.

—D&C 84:46

"Our spirits were pure and holy when they entered our tabernacles," taught Brigham Young (*Journal of Discourses*, 8:138). Thus the newborn child instinctively cleaves to that which is right and good. Indeed, the revealed word attests that "every spirit of man was innocent in the beginning; and God having redeemed man from the fall, men became again, in their infant state, innocent before God. And that wicked one cometh and *taketh away light and truth, through disobedience,* from the children of men, and because of the tradition of their fathers." (D&C 93:38–39, italics added.) Given that the devil cannot take that which we do not have, we conclude that a child is born with a divine inheritance of light and truth—an inheritance that can be added to or taken from. Since disobedience and allegiance to false traditions result in the loss of this heavenly endowment, it is evident that obedience and devotion to truth enhance it.

The Light of Christ

Though a veil is drawn over our minds at the time we come into this world, we retain a certain sense and feel for that which we once knew. Paul said that even those born of gentile lineage have "the law written in their hearts" and that they "do by nature the things contained in the law" (Romans 2:14–15). "The Spirit," we are told, "giveth light to every man that cometh into the world; and the Spirit enlighteneth every man through the world, that hearkeneth to the voice of the Spirit. And every one that hearkeneth to the voice of the Spirit cometh unto God, even the Father." (D&C 84:46–47.) Again, the Savior testified, "I am the true light that lighteth every man that cometh into the world" (D&C 93:2). Mormon explained that "the Spirit of Christ is given to every man, that he may know good from evil" (Moroni 7:16).

Born with a Testimony

Within the household of faith, among those who have what we call "believing blood," we expect to find people naturally inclined to believe the principles of salvation. "Since much of Israel has been scattered among the Gentile nations, it follows that millions of people have mixed blood, blood that is part Israel and part Gentile. The more of the blood of Israel that an individual has, the easier it is for him to believe the message of salvation as taught by the authorized agents of the Lord. This principle is the one our Lord had in mind when he said to certain Jews: 'I am the good shepherd, and know my sheep, and *am known of mine.* . . . But ye believe not, because ye are not of my sheep, as I said unto you. *My sheep hear my voice,* and I know them, and *they follow me.*' (John 10:14, 26–27.)" (Bruce R. McConkie, *Mormon Doctrine,* p. 81.)

Thus it is that some are born with a special capacity to know and recognize the truth. We refer to them as having believing blood, having in mind the idea that in the pre-earth life they developed a propensity for truth, or a talent to recognize the verities of heaven and a desire to live righteously. Such are the "elect" that the Savior said would "hear my voice and harden not their hearts" (D&C 29:7). These are they who hear the voice of testimony, the voice of good doctrine, the voice of righteousness, the voice of salvation.

Awakening to the Things of the Spirit

We traditionally describe those who are born outside the Church and who subsequently join it as *converts*, implying that they turned from another belief to embrace the testimony of the Restoration. In fact, this is rarely the case. In most instances, those who have joined the Church tell us: "There was no conversion. Everything the missionaries told me I already believed!" That which we call conversion may more aptly be described as an awakening, a distant memory, or an echo from the past. "People ask me why I left my old church," the so-called convert said. "I tell them it was not a matter of my leaving my old church, but rather a matter of my coming home."

In general, creedal religions define God as a spirit essence—a being without body, parts, or passions. Yet when missionaries tell their investigators that God is a personal being, that he has body, parts, and passions, and that when they pray they ought to see in their mind's eye a loving Father, frequently no objection is raised. Generally the response is, "Well, that is what I have always done." In like manner, when we announce to our nonmember friends that marriage is meant to be eternal and that heaven would hardly be heaven if we were not reunited with our families and spouses, the typical response is, "Well, that is what I have always thought."

People who are unencumbered by the traditions of their fathers have an innate sense for truth. It is not uncommon for gospel teachers to spend many hours in prayerful study, seeking answers to difficult questions, only to have their students casually accept those answers as if they had always known them. "That's the way I always understood it," a student might say. And yet the teacher is quite confident that those so saying had never given the matter a moment's thought before it was brought up in class. This is simply a manifestation of the verity that we are not learning these things for the first time; the truths of salvation have a familiar spirit, a spirit that is often immediately recognizable to those who once knew them.

And what of those born in the faith? They are born with a testimony; it is their rightful inheritance. Peter promised those who would repent and be baptized that they would receive a remission of sins along with the Holy Ghost, which promise, he said, "is unto you, and to your children, and to all [having reference to their posterity] that are afar off" (Acts 2:38–39). Commenting on this text, Joseph Smith said: "The promise was to extend by lineage; for Peter says, not only unto you, but 'to your children, and to all that are afar off.' From this we infer, that the promise was to continue unto their children's children, and even unto as many as the Lord their God should call," or from generation to generation. (*Teachings of the Prophet Joseph Smith,* p. 81.)

Our children "are entitled to the Spirit of the Gospel from their mothers' wombs; they have it with them all the time; they are born in it," Brigham Young taught. They do not know they possess the light of the Holy Spirit, he explained, until they leave home and go out into the world and see the contrast. "They hear their fathers pray, and they hear the Apostles and Prophets preach, but they cannot know that 'Mormonism' is true for themselves until they have had the privilege of being placed in circumstances to exercise faith for themselves, and to pray to God for themselves for testimony and knowledge. Then they obtain the power of the Holy Spirit, which *awakens their senses,* and they know for themselves that God lives, for he hears and answers their prayers." (*Journal of Discourses,* 11:215, italics added.)

Recognizing Truth

Moroni sealed the Book of Mormon with the promise that the honest truth seeker could know of its truthfulness by the power of the Holy Ghost. "And by the power of the Holy Ghost ye may know the truth of all things," he asserted (Moroni 10:5). This is not to say that those who have received the Holy Ghost know all truth, or even that they can obtain it by the spirit of revelation. To have a full knowledge of all things would defeat the purpose of mortality. It is requisite that in this sphere some questions go unanswered and some things remain unexplained. Nevertheless those who have received the gift of the Holy Ghost have received the promise that they, by that power, can in all instances be worthy of divine direction to discern between truth and error. The principle finds expression in a revelation given to Hyrum Smith. To him the Lord said, "I will impart unto you of my Spirit, which shall enlighten your mind, which shall fill your soul with joy; and then shall ye know, or by this shall you know, all things whatsoever you desire of me, which are pertaining unto things of righteousness, in faith believing in me that you shall receive" (D&C 11:13–14).

It is noticeable that in our day, when wickedness is so rampant, frequently those who support the cause of error and sin are extremely articulate. They advocate with great sophistry what to Latter-day Saints is clearly the adversary's cause, making good appear as evil, and evil appear as good (see 2 Nephi 28:16, 20). They persistently press their aims under either the pretended or misguided claim of loyalty to an acknowledged standard—in the United States, to the First Amendment, to women's rights, or to individual freedoms—having long ago learned the value of marching at the side of a good cause. We may not be able to match their witchery of words; we may not be able to refute their twisted logic or to see how they have distorted their sources. Such is not necessary in order for us to know that what they say and what they do is not right. We have a sense and a feel for truth. We know that spirit that is apostolic and that spirit that is not.

Joseph Smith said that truth tastes good. "I can taste the principles of eternal life," he said, "and so can you. They are given to me by the revelations of Jesus Christ; and I know that when I tell you these words of eternal life as they are given to me, you taste them, and I know that you believe them. You say honey is sweet, and so do I. I can also taste the spirit of eternal life. I know it is good; and when I tell you of these things which were given me by inspiration of the Holy Spirit, you are bound to receive them as sweet, and rejoice more and more." (*Teachings of the Prophet Joseph Smith,* p. 355.) We need not know all things. If we can discern that which is sweet to the taste from that which is bitter we can ignore all the clever advertising and confidently do what is right.

There is a quiet confidence that comes to those acquainted with the things of the Spirit. This is especially evident in the leading councils of the Church. The Brethren have neither the time, the energy, nor even the expertise, in some instances, to solve all the problems or respond to all the questions that face them. They freely delegate the finding of solutions to others. What they retain to themselves is the confirmation that those decisions are right. What they are saying, in effect, is, "You figure it out and we will know if you are right." Thus it is not required that they know all things, nor is it required that they do all things; but only that they properly discern all things of serious moment to the Church or the welfare of the Saints.

This same power of discernment should be shared by every member of the Church. When bad doctrine is taught and espoused as eternal truth, for instance, the members of the Church have the same capacity to discern it as do their leaders. President Joseph F. Smith explained that this is because members of the Church know truth for themselves. They stand independent. "They have learned it in the school of experience, as well as by the gift and power of the Holy Ghost." Thus President Smith concluded that no man, nor set of men, can lead this people from the paths of rectitude, righteousness, and faith in the restored gospel. "It can't be done. Why? Because [the members of the Church] know the principles of the gospel, as well as their leaders do." (Conference Report, October 1910, pp. 127–28.) They have entered into the same covenants and received the same promises as their leaders. Whatever outpouring of the Spirit the leadership is entitled to, the Saints have equal claim upon.

Spiritual Impulses

To be responsive to the spirit of revelation is to be responsive to our feelings. Joseph Smith said, "All things whatsoever God in his infinite wisdom has seen fit and proper to reveal to us, while we are dwelling in mortality, in regard to our mortal bodies, are revealed to us in the abstract," revealed "as though we had no [mortal] bodies at all" (*Teachings of the Prophet Joseph Smith*, p. 355). Describing this process, Spencer W. Kimball said: "Learning the language of prayer is a joyous, lifetime experience. Sometimes ideas flood our mind as we listen after our prayers. Sometimes feelings press upon us. A spirit of calmness assures us that all will be well. But always, if we have been honest and earnest, we will experience a good feeling—a feeling of warmth for our Father in Heaven and a sense of his love for us." ("Pray Always," p. 5.) George Q. Cannon said it thus: "I will tell you a rule by which you may know the Spirit of God from the spirit of evil. The Spirit of God always produces joy and satisfaction of mind. When you have that Spirit you are happy; when you have another spirit you are not happy. The spirit of doubt is the spirit of the evil one; it produces uneasiness and other feelings that interfere with happiness and peace." (*Journal of Discourses,* 15:375.)

"The Spirit does not get our attention by shouting or shaking us with a heavy hand," said Elder Boyd K. Packer. "Rather it whispers. It caresses so gently that if we are preoccupied we may not feel it at all." (*"That All May Be Edified,"* p. 336.) "The work of righteousness shall be peace," Isaiah said, "and the effect of righteousness quietness and assurance for ever" (Isaiah 32:17). James put it in this way: "The wisdom that is from above is first pure, then peaceable, gentle, and easy to be intreated, full of mercy and good fruits, without partiality, and without hypocrisy. And the fruit of righteousness is sown in peace of them that make peace." (James 3:17–18.)

The Susceptibility of Women to the Spirit

Because the spirit of revelation is so closely associated with the feelings of the heart, because the voice of the Spirit is the voice of gentleness, because the Spirit is naturally attracted to purity, and because the Lord delights to honor those who serve him—especially those with whom he has entrusted the care of innocent and newly born children—it stands to reason that women are, by their very nature, more susceptible to the spirit of revelation than are men.

It is natural for man to acquire—to subdue, to confront, to battle, to obtain dominion over things. It is natural for the woman to give, to be gentle and compassionate (though the Master's teachings and example make these traits also proper for men). Obviously those latter characteristics are more likely to attract the heaven-sent voice. Keys, power, authority, priesthood—these have been given to men. The miracle of copartnership with God in clothing his spirit children with physical bodies has been given to women. It is for man to protect life; it is for woman to give life. As the body of the unborn child takes its strength and nourishment from its mother, so must the spirit of that child, in like manner, be nourished and strengthened by the mortal mother if it too is to grow healthy and strong. Her faith then will tend to become its faith, her strength its strength. The father will preside when the family kneels to pray, but it will be the mother who has taught the children how to pray.

"Little children," the scriptures declare, "are holy" (D&C 74:7). We are sanctified by their presence. When the disciples sought to prevent loving mothers from bringing their little children to the Savior, he responded, "Suffer little children, and forbid them not, to come unto me: for of such is the kingdom of heaven" (Matthew 19:14). Could it be that Christ is suggesting not just that those who inhabit the celestial world will have the innocence, submissiveness, and purity of children, as we have traditionally said, but that heaven would hardly be heaven without little children? Does not godhood center in the doctrine of fatherhood and motherhood? Is it not the doctrine of eternal increase? (See D&C 131:4.) And if such is the nature of heaven, perhaps there is no more perfect setting for the outpouring of the Spirit than one in which a loving mother takes her little child in her arms to nestle the child and speak of future dreams. And again in future years as that child grows to maturity, who more than his mother is entitled to the whisperings of the Spirit—its promptings and impulses—to bless and protect the child? Surely heaven's light shines most brightly upon mothers.

The Holy Ghost and the Priesthood

The Melchizedek Priesthood "is the channel through which all knowledge, doctrine, the plan of salvation and every important matter is revealed from heaven," Joseph Smith taught. It is, he said, "the channel through which the Almighty commenced revealing His glory at the beginning of the creation of this earth, and through which He has continued to reveal Himself to the children of men to the present time, and through which He will make known His purposes to the end of time." (*Teachings of the Prophet Joseph Smith,* pp. 166–67.) Revelation affirms that "this greater priesthood administereth the gospel and holdeth the key of the mysteries of the kingdom, even the key of the knowledge of God" (D&C 84:19). Thus the Aaronic Priesthood may baptize with water, but only the Melchizedek Priesthood can confer "the baptism of fire and the Holy Ghost" (D&C 20:41, 43, 46).

Of necessity, the profession of priesthood must carry with it the profession of revelation. Oliver Cowdery reasoned thus: "The question might be asked, have men authority to administer in the name of Christ, who deny revelations, when His testimony is no less than the spirit of prophecy, and His religion based, built, and sustained by immediate revelations, in all ages of the world when He has had a people on earth?" (*Messenger and Advocate* 1 [October 1834]: 14–16.) If we understand priesthood to be the power and authority by which men act in the name of God, then to profess priesthood is to profess communion with God; for how else could we properly act in his name? A priesthood that professes no revelation — a priesthood that claims the heavens are sealed — is as a fire without light, a fire without warmth.

Conclusion

The companionship of the Holy Ghost and the attendant spirit of revelation are the rightful inheritance of the household of faith. That Spirit is so natural to those who have been born and raised in the environs of faith and righteousness that it goes almost unnoticed.

It is more powerful in expanding the mind, enlightening the understanding, and storing the intellect with present knowledge, of a man who is of the literal seed of Abraham, than one that is a Gentile, though it may not have half as much visible effect upon the body; for as the Holy Ghost falls upon one of the literal seed of Abraham, it is calm and serene; and his whole soul and body are only exercised by the pure spirit of intelligence; while the effect of the Holy Ghost upon a Gentile, is to purge out the old blood, and make him actually of the seed of Abraham. That man that has none of the blood of Abraham (naturally) must have a new creation by the Holy Ghost. In such a case, there may be more of a powerful effect upon the body, and visible to the eye, than upon an Israelite, while the Israelite at first might be far before the Gentile in pure intelligence. (*Teachings of the Prophet Joseph Smith,* pp. 149–50.)

6

The Gifts of the Spirit

Every man hath his proper gift of God, one after this
manner, and another after that.
— *1 Corinthians 7:7*

The wisdom of God is manifest in the gifts he gives his children
and in the manner in which these gifts are given. Heaven's gifts,
though freely given, are only granted to those worthy and prepared
to receive them. Any other system would profane that which is sacred and make mockery of the powers of heaven. Only those who
have been cleansed of sin in the waters of baptism and who have
been promised the companionship of the Holy Ghost by the laying
on of hands are heirs to these sacred gifts. They are not for the
world or the worldly; they are not for infants nor for the spiritually
immature; they are not granted on the basis of tenure in the
Church or because one has been called to a certain office or position—though such callings may bring an increased claim upon
them. Rather, they are dispensed at heaven's choosing to those
keeping the commandments and those seeking earnestly so to do
(D&C 46:9). Indeed, every faithful citizen of the kingdom of God
has the promised assurance that a spiritual endowment is his or
hers, though it may lie latent within the soul until the proper time
of expression calls it forth.

The Community of the Saints

It is an eternal verity that in the realm of spiritual things we reap as we have sown. Those who enjoy a rich harvest of the fruits of the Spirit are those who have spent long hours laboring in the Lord's vineyard. Spiritual strength comes from spiritual labor, the fruits of the Spirit from the well-tended plant. The vineyard and the fruit are the Lord's, and we are but stewards or servants. Thus our revelation declares that the fruits of the Spirit "are given unto the church" (D&C 46:10). We understand this to mean that notwithstanding the fact that all spiritual endowments are personal or individual, it is intended that they be used for the enlightenment, edification, and blessing of the congregation of the Saints.

"These gifts are infinite in number and endless in their manifestations because God himself is infinite and endless, and because the needs of those who receive them are as numerous, varied, and different as there are people in the kingdom" (Bruce R. McConkie, *A New Witness for the Articles of Faith,* p. 270). "To some is given one, and to some is given another, that all may be profited thereby." The genius of this system of divine distribution of gifts is that all of us are in a position to be instructed, blessed, and edified by others. None of us can enjoy a fulness of the outpourings of the Spirit in isolation of the body of the Saints. We must meet together often simply because "all have not every gift given." (D&C 46:11, 12; 1 Corinthians 12:4.) Each of us is in a position in which we can be instructed or otherwise blessed by others. And of equal importance, each of us—from the greatest to the least—has something to contribute, something that others cannot do as well as we can. To illustrate the point and to give us an idea as to the nature of the gifts bequeathed by the Spirit, we will turn to Doctrine and Covenants section 46.

"To some it is given by the Holy Ghost," we are told, "to know that Jesus Christ is the Son of God, and that he was crucified for the sins of the world. To others it is given to believe on their words, that they also might have eternal life if they continue faithful." (D&C 46:13–14.) This is not to say that some few of our number are to have a testimony that Jesus is the Christ and the rest of us are to believe on their testimony. All must know by the witness of the Spirit that Jesus is the Christ if they are to profess a testimony; and surely all who have claim upon citizenship in the kingdom of heaven must have this personal witness of the Spirit. What it does say is that some have a witness of this saving truth that goes beyond that which is experienced by the generality of faithful Saints. Indeed, testimony in its formative stage draws strength from and builds upon the more seasoned and mature witness of others.

There are those in every dispensation to whom the Lord has manifest himself, those whom he has called and chosen to be special witnesses of him. These have the gift of testifying of him, the special spiritual endowment to bear a witness of him with a power that raises the spiritual level of a meeting or a conference. Others have a special capacity to hear and feel that testimony, and by it can know with the same confidence and assurance of the reality of Christ's divine sonship as does the one graced with the privilege of being a special witness. All are to be witnesses of Christ, but some have been so blessed as to be special witnesses of him.

Continuing with the revelation, we are told that "to some it is given by the Holy Ghost to know the differences of administration," that is, to understand the varieties of service or pastoral care needed among a particular congregation. This ensures that those in need receive help at the appropriate time and place or, as the scripture states, "suiting his mercies according to the conditions of the children of men." (D&C 46:15.) "Again," the Lord said, "it is given by the Holy Ghost to some to know the diversities of operations, whether they be of God, that the manifestations of the Spirit may be given to every man to profit withal" (D&C 46:16; 1 Corinthians 12:7). "It is to the gift of discernment that reference is here made. Appointed leaders must be able to divide true doctrine from false, to single out true prophets from the false, to discern between true spirits and false ones." (Bruce R. McConkie, *A New Witness for the Articles of Faith*, p. 278.) Thus, we are assured that the Spirit will manifest itself in a variety of ways to the edification and blessing of all who seek it.

Among the specific gifts promised are those of wisdom and knowledge, not the wisdom of the world or the knowledge of man but "hidden wisdom, which God ordained before the world unto our glory" (1 Corinthians 2:7), and "great treasures of knowledge, even hidden treasures'' (D&C 89:19). Thus, ours becomes the wisdom and knowledge of the Spirit, that divine endowment of "light which shineth in darkness, and the darkness comprehendeth it not'' (D&C 6:21). Such was the wisdom that Joseph Smith obtained in the Sacred Grove and the knowledge he obtained through the restoration of the holy priesthood, which "priesthood administereth the gospel and holdeth the key of the mysteries of the kingdom, even the key of the knowledge of God'' (D&C 84:19). The Melchizedek Priesthood, he said, was the "channel through which all knowledge, doctrine, the plan of salvation and every important matter is revealed from heaven'' (*Teachings of the Prophet Joseph Smith*, p. 167).

"And again, to some it is given to have faith to be healed; and to others it is given to have faith to heal'' (D&C 46:19-20). As the Saints have been given the power to bless one another spiritually, so they have been given the power to bless one another physically. Of those who have received the gift of the Holy Ghost through the waters of baptism and who magnify their priesthood callings, the Lord said: "In my name they shall do many wonderful works; in my name they shall cast out devils; in my name they shall heal the sick; in my name they shall open the eyes of the blind, and unstop the ears of the deaf; and the tongue of the dumb shall speak; and if any man shall administer poison unto them it shall not hurt them; and the poison of a serpent shall not have power to harm them'' (D&C 84:66-72).

"And again, to some it is given the working of miracles'' (D&C 46:21). In the spiritual sense miracles are occurrences which are beyond the powers of mortal men to perform. Literally the word *miracle* means "wonder'' or "wonderful work.'' Prophecies of the restoration of the gospel in the last days refer to it as "a marvelous work and a wonder.'' Truly the restoration of the gospel and the coming forth of the Book of Mormon are miracles, for both are beyond the capacity of mortal men to bring to pass. The greatest miracle to precede the Second Coming will be the manner in which the gospel will go to those of every nation, kindred, tongue, and people. There are and will be those in virtually every congregation of the Saints who will be blessed with the gift of miracles. To such is granted the spiritual power to cause things to happen that defy the limitations of mortal men.

"And to others it is given to prophesy" (D&C 46:22). To prophesy is to declare the mind of God; it is to teach the saving principles of the gospel of Christ by the power of the Holy Ghost. The role of a prophet is to be the covenant spokesman, which role he fills by declaring faith, repentance, and baptism, and by giving all other admonition necessary for the salvation of the children of men. Prophecy embraces the foretelling of future events, but certainly is not limited to it. There was, for example, "never a greater prophet born of a woman" than John the Baptist (*Teachings of the Prophet Joseph Smith,* p. 261), and yet he made no prophecies save the coming of Christ. Hopefully, there are those among every congregation of the Saints who are imbued with the spirit of prophecy, and thus those who can preach and teach the principles of the gospel by the power of the Spirit. And hopefully, there are those in addition to our patriarchs who can, as is necessary, foretell that portion of future events that are expedient for us to know in order that we be properly prepared in all things.

"And to others the discerning of spirits" (D&C 46:23). The gift of discernment is frequently associated with the office of bishop, for the bishop must function as a judge in Israel (D&C 46:27). This gift is also associated with the office of President of the Church, for he must protect the Saints against false Christs, false prophets, and false doctrines (D&C 107:91–92). It is a gift also granted to inspired teachers and parents to protect the rising generation as they grow to spiritual maturity. Satan is the arch-deceiver, consummate counterfeiter, great imposter, and peddler of cheap imitations of every correct and good thing. Those with the gift of discernment are as the watchmen upon the tower who guard the safety of the community.

"And again, it is given to some to speak with tongues; and to another is given the interpretation of tongues" (D&C 46:24–25). "Three manifestations of the gift of 'speaking in tongues' are evident in God's dealings with his children: (1) speaking the pure Adamic language (Moses 6:6, 46) . . . (2) speaking a foreign but known tongue (Acts 2:2, 4–6); and (3) speaking by the power of the Holy Ghost.'' (Joseph Fielding McConkie and Robert L. Millet, *Doctrinal Commentary on the Book of Mormon*, 1:369–70.) The gift of tongues, which was granted on the day of Pentecost in order that devout men of all nations might hear the gospel preached according to their own understanding, performs that same function today. Its manifestation is not uncommon in temples where language difficulties could prevent various people from understanding the promises of the Lord, in missionary work among the nations of the earth, and in the protection and preservation of the Saints as circumstances require them to travel in strange lands. This gift also manifests itself in the remarkable facility with which young missionaries learn foreign tongues, and in the manner in which the Spirit speaks through them. The most frequent manifestation of the interpretation of tongues is the manner in which those who have properly attuned themselves with the Spirit can hear and understand a message in greater clarity than that in which it was given.

"And all these gifts come from God, for the benefit of the children of God" (D&C 46:26). Such are the gifts of the Spirit, and such are their purposes in granting everyone of the household of faith a role in edifying, blessing, and strengthening their fellow Saints. Thus Paul cites them as the crowning argument to sustain the need for unity among the Saints.

> For by one Spirit are we all baptized into one body, whether we be Jews or Gentiles, whether we be bond or free; and have been all made to drink into one Spirit.
>
> For the body is not one member, but many.
>
> If the foot shall say, Because I am not the hand, I am not of the body; is it therefore not of the body?
>
> And if the ear shall say, Because I am not the eye, I am not of the body; is it therefore not of the body?
>
> If the whole body were an eye, where were the hearing? If the whole were hearing, where were the smelling?
>
> But now hath God set the members every one of them in the body, as it hath pleased him.
>
> And if they were all one member, where were the body?
>
> But now are they many members, yet but one body.

And the eye cannot say unto the hand, I have no need of thee: nor again the head to the feet, I have no need of you.

Nay, much more those members of the body, which seem to be more feeble, are necessary:

And those members of the body, which we think to be less honourable, upon these we bestow more abundant honour; and our uncomely parts have more abundant comeliness.

For our comely parts have no need: but God hath tempered the body together, having given more abundant honour to that part which lacked;

That there should be no schism in the body; but that the members should have the same care one for another.

And whether one member suffer, all the members suffer with it; or one member be honoured, all the members rejoice with it.

Now ye are the body of Christ, and members in particular. (1 Corinthians 12:13–27.)

There Are No Limits to the Gifts of God

As there are no limits to the gifts that loving fathers may desire to give their children, so there are no limits to the gifts that our Eternal Father can give those of his children who love and honor him (see Luke 11:13). We would no more seek to place a limit on the number of spiritual gifts than we would seek to seal the heavens and tell God that he can no longer speak or manifest himself to those worthy of his presence. Spiritual gifts are as diverse and as countless as the manifestations of faith and are as rich and as diverse as the fruits of the earth. Those mentioned in the scriptures are but illustrations or examples. Where the Doctrine and Covenants speaks of the gift of wisdom and the gift of knowledge, Moroni speaks of the gift of teaching wisdom and teaching knowledge (Moroni 10:9–10). Moroni thus indicates teaching to be a spiritual gift and suggests that some have a spiritual talent in one dimension of teaching, while others have talent in other areas. For instance, some, particularly among the sisters, have a special talent to teach little children, among whom they work miracles of faith, while others have a special capacity or talent to teach adults. Each succeeds in the area of his or her gift in a marvelous manner. But were we to have them change roles, they could well find themselves with feelings of complete inadequacy.

To the list enumerated in the Doctrine and Covenants, Moroni also adds "exceedingly great faith" (Moroni 10:11), thereby suggesting that though faith is a blessing of the Spirit to be shared by all Latter-day Saints, some have it in greater measure than others. We could liken this and other gifts to the worship of God through the singing of hymns. All are expected to join in the congregational singing, while only one may be invited to sing a solo because of special talents that are his or hers. With that special talent with which he or she has been graced comes the increased ability to raise the spiritual level of our meetings. So it is with faith and other like gifts. All have them in some measure, while some few have a particular gift in greater measure than the generality of Saints, and thus have a special capacity to make a unique contribution that is enjoyed by all.

Moroni also stated that some have the capacity to "work mighty miracles," while others have the gift of prophecy whereby they can "prophesy concerning all things." To still others, he declared, is given the gift of "the beholding of angels and ministering spirits." Surely this is an experience that many have sought and not received. Moroni is simply suggesting that it is a spiritual gift, like that of teaching, preaching, or the gift of healing, that has been granted particularly to some. When speaking of the gift of tongues he notes that some have the gift to interpret many different languages, and that some enjoy "divers kinds of tongues." (Moroni 10:11-16.)

The great diversity of gifts means that the absence of any member of the congregation is a loss to every member of the congregation. As Paul said, when one member suffers all suffer, and when one member is honored all are honored. For a member of the Church to refuse to fellowship with the body of the Saints is for him or her to deprive the community of the Saints of the blessing of his or her particular gift or gifts. The gifts of the Spirit are given to be shared, and for someone to fail to do so is for him to withhold an inheritance rightfully belonging to the whole family of faith. "The body hath need of every member, that all may be edified together, that the system may be kept perfect" (D&C 84:110).

Seek Ye Earnestly the Best Gifts

The scriptural injunction is that we seek earnestly to obtain the best gifts (D&C 46:8). A more colorful expression comes to us from Paul, who enjoined us to "covet earnestly the best gifts" (1 Corinthians 12:31). This, of course, raises the question as to which gifts are "the best gifts" and why God, who is no respecter of persons, would give to some better gifts than to others? A proper response, it seems, would be that the "best gifts" are those which are "best" for us personally by which to magnify the offices and callings that are ours, or the "best" to respond to the particular circumstances and needs that exist in our present situations. Apart from particular needs, however, some gifts are indeed greater than others. Joseph Smith suggested that quiet gifts, those gifts that could go unobserved, were generally greater than the more obtrusive or visible gifts.

Suppose, for instance, that someone were to stand in a fast and testimony meeting and speak in tongues and another stand and interpret. Their doing so would cause considerable excitement among the congregation and would be remembered and spoken of for years to come. By contrast, suppose the same two men were to stand and teach saving principles by the power of the Spirit. Would there be the same sense of excitement? Would people remember the occasion and speak of it with special fondness in years to come? Or would many who had been present go their way without any particular sensitivity that something very special had taken place? In response to such queries, Joseph Smith observed:

> The word of wisdom, and the word of knowledge, are as much gifts as any other, yet if a person possessed both of these gifts, or received them by the imposition of hands, who would know it? Another might receive the gift of faith, and

they would be as ignorant of it. Or suppose a man had the gift of healing or power to work miracles, that would not then be known; it would require time and circumstances to call these gifts into operation. Suppose a man had the discerning of spirits, who would be the wiser of it? Or if he had the interpretation of tongues, unless someone spoke in an unknown tongue, he of course would have to be silent; there are only two gifts that could be made visible—the gift of tongues and the gift of prophecy. These are things that are the most talked about, and yet if a person spoke in an unknown tongue, according to Paul's testimony, he would be a barbarian to those present. They would say that it was gibberish; and if he prophesied they would call it nonsense. The gift of tongues is the smallest gift perhaps of the whole, and yet it is one that is the most sought after.

So that according to the testimony of Scripture and the manifestations of the Spirit in ancient days, very little could be known about it by the surrounding multitude, except on some extraordinary occasion, as on the day of Pentecost.

The greatest, the best, and the most useful gifts would be known nothing about by an observer. It is true that a man might prophesy, which is a great gift, and one that Paul told the people—the Church—to seek after and to covet, rather than to speak in tongues; but what does the world know about prophesying? Paul says that it "serveth only to those that believe." But does not the Scripture say that they spake in tongues and prophesied? Yes; but who is it that writes these Scriptures? Not the men of the world or mere casual observers, but the Apostles—men who knew one gift from another, and of course were capable of writing about it; if we had the testimony of the Scribes and Pharisees concerning the outpouring of the Spirit on the day of Pentecost, they would have told us that it was no gift, but that the people were "drunken with new wine," and we shall finally have to come to the same conclusion that Paul did—"No man knows the things of God but by the Spirit of God;" for with the great revelations of Paul when he was caught up into the third heaven and saw things that were not lawful to utter, no man was apprised of it until he mentioned it himself fourteen years after; and when John had the curtains of heaven withdrawn, and by vision looked through the dark vista of future ages, and contemplated events that should transpire throughout every subsequent period of time, until the final winding up scene — while he gazed upon the glories of the eternal world, saw an innumerable company of angels and heard the voice of God — it was in the Spirit, on the Lord's day, unnoticed and unobserved by the world. (*Teachings of the Prophet Joseph Smith*, pp. 246-47.)

It is important that a distinction be made between sign seekers and truth seekers, between those who plead for proof and those who are earnestly seeking spiritual gifts. The distinction can be clearly made: one is born of impurity and the other of purity; one is an announcement of doubt, while the other is an expression of faith; one is evidence of a profligate drone, and the other of a profitable servant. The sign seeker promises faithfulness if sufficient evidence is given that faith is no longer required. Those properly seeking spiritual gifts plant the seed of faith and patiently tend it, awaiting a day of maturation and then the day of harvest. These understand that the fruits of the Spirit are given for the benefit of those who love the Lord and make an honest effort to keep all his commandments.

Spiritual gifts are not given as a sign for those who seek to "consume it upon their lusts" (D&C 46:9), meaning that they are not given to gratify curiosity in the realm of sacred things. The matter of what gifts we ought to seek is most often determined by need. Those called on foreign missions ought to seek the gift of tongues; a bishop ought to seek the gift of discernment; the sick or afflicted might seek the gift to be healed; and so forth. The gifts of the Spirit are most appropriately sought when our purpose is to bless others with them.

How We Identify the Gifts That Are Ours

When we study the revelations on spiritual gifts the question is often asked, "How can I know what my particular gift is?" Since a primary purpose of spiritual gifts is to bless and edify others, it

naturally follows that as we fill the callings that we are given and
labor in the offices to which we are called, we will have opportunity to become familiar with the spiritual talents that are ours. Particular circumstances call forth particular gifts. If someone has the
gift of healing it will not manifest itself until someone is sick; if
someone else has the gift of interpretation of tongues, as the
Prophet noted, it will go unknown until there is something that
needs to be interpreted. In some instances special gifts that are
ours will be identified in patriarchal blessings, fathers' blessings,
ordinations, or when we are being set apart for offices or callings.

It ought also to be observed that though we are granted gifts of
the Spirit by God, we are not excused from the responsibility to
nurture and develop them. The gift of teaching serves as an example. To be granted the gift is one thing, but to develop and use it
quite another. Gifts, like talents, are not exhausted by use but
rather enhanced. Like a muscle, the gift is strengthened through its
exercise.

Gifts Associated with Special Stewardships

Some gifts are obviously associated with offices. The testimony
that Jesus is the Christ is associated with the calling of Apostle, the
gift of understanding differences of administration is associated
with a position of presidency, the gift of discerning is associated
with the office of bishop, and so forth. Such gifts may be sur-
rendered when a release comes. A bishop, for instance, may have
the capacity to read the troubled heart—something that would be
quite improper for him to do following his release. Indeed, we are
told that unto some it is given to be able to discern all gifts "lest
there shall be any among you professing and yet be not of God"
(D&C 46:27).

It is granted to the man who stands at the head of the church to
possess all gifts "in order that every member may be profited
thereby" (D&C 46:29). In so saying, however, it need not be supposed that the President of the Church has all gifts in their perfection, or that he has them in greater measure than everyone else in
the Church, or that every President of the Church has each gift in

the same proportion as every other man who ever presided over the Church. Each of our prophets has brought to the prophetic office particular talents which were in particular need at that particular time. Yet each of them has been blessed by the spiritual strength of good counselors and by the rich storehouse of gifts that always exists among the members of the leading quorums of the Church.

Conclusion

Spiritual gifts are a sign of the true Church and have been so in every gospel dispensation. Any people who have been properly baptized and who have had hands laid upon their heads for the gift of the Holy Ghost will also be the recipients of spiritual gifts. As spiritual gifts are a sign of the true Church, so they are a sign by which we may know those who are true to the Church. If the gifts of the Spirit are not visible in our lives, if they are not operative in our families, then appropriate changes are needed in order that the Holy Ghost will once again become our companion (Moroni 7:35–39).

Spiritual gifts are the perfect system whereby the Lord has chosen to bind those of faith together in an interdependent community, one in which everyone can contribute to the strength and beauty of its fabric. There are none who have the companionship of the Holy Ghost who are without the ability and power to make a significant contribution to the kingdom of God. None such are without reason to praise God, to recognize their special gifts as an evidence of his goodness and as a testimony of the reality of his gospel (D&C 88:33).

7

Symbols of the Holy Ghost

*The sign of the dove was instituted before the crea-
tion of the world, a witness for the Holy Ghost, and
the devil cannot come in the sign of a dove.*
—*Joseph Smith*

Because the languages of men cannot do justice to the glories of
heaven, the scriptures frequently draw upon the richer and more
expressive language of symbolism to describe eternal truths. It is
both natural and appropriate that the language of symbolism be
used to teach us about the members of the Godhead and about
their various roles in the salvation of men. Let us consider symbols
commonly used in the scriptures to represent and teach us about
the Holy Ghost.

The Sign of the Dove

When Jesus of Nazareth came up out of the waters of baptism,
John saw the heavens opened "and he saw the Spirit of God de-
scending like a dove and lighting upon Jesus" (JST, Matthew
3:45). In this instance, says the King James Version, "the Holy
Ghost descended in a bodily shape like a dove" (Luke 3:22); that
is, the Holy Ghost, who "has not a body of flesh and bones, but is
a personage of spirit" (D&C 130:22), made his presence manifest
by the sign of a dove. "The sign of the dove [and indeed a dove
would have been literally present at the baptism of Jesus] was in-

stituted before the creation of the world, a witness for the Holy Ghost, and the devil cannot come in the sign of a dove. The Holy Ghost is a personage, and is in the form of a personage. It does not confine itself to the *form* of the dove, but in *sign* of the dove. The Holy Ghost cannot be transformed into a dove; but the sign of a dove was given to John to signify the truth of the deed, as the dove is an emblem or token of truth and innocence." (*Teachings of the Prophet Joseph Smith,* p. 276.)

The dove, which is a universal symbol for peace, has been a sign or token of the presence of the Holy Ghost among prophets and righteous people of all ages (see Abraham, facsimile 2, figure 7). When Noah sought to know if the waters were dried up from off the earth (for it was the design of the Lord to cleanse it from all that was unclean and unworthy of his presence), he sent forth a dove, and "the dove came in to him in the evening; and, lo, in her mouth was an olive leaf pluckt off: so Noah knew that the waters were abated from off the earth" (Genesis 8:11), and that it was again a fit place to be inhabited by the pure and innocent.

Fire

From the beginning of history fire has been associated with warmth and light. In the theophanies recorded in the scriptures, fire frequently represents God's holiness and glory. Beginning in the day of Adam, fire consumed the sacrificial offering as a token of divine approval (Moses 5:5). The ever-burning fire on the altar of the tabernacle in the wilderness (Leviticus 6:12-13) was first kindled from heaven, and was so rekindled at the dedication of Solomon's temple (Leviticus 9:13, 24; 2 Chronicles 7:1-3). Fire was a symbol of Jehovah's presence and the instrument of his power, by which he manifested approval or brought destruction upon the rebellious (Exodus 3:2-5; Numbers 11:1-3). Describing the role of fire as a symbol of the divine presence, Orson Pratt observed:

> Moses was baptized with the Holy Ghost and with fire, so that when he came down from mount Sinai, after being with the Lord many days, his face shone with that brilliancy that

the children of Israel could not endure the brightness and intensity of the light, but fled and stood afar off. Moses was obliged to veil his face to hide the glory of his countenance from Israel. It is this same fire that has so often been exhibited by holy angels, when they have appeared in their glory to mortals. It was this same fire that rested upon the tabernacle and camp of Israel, for forty years in the wilderness. It was this same fire that broke forth among the rebellious ones, and consumed them by thousands. It was this same fire that consumed the sacrifice offered by Elijah, and even consumed the stones of the altar and great quantities of water, poured upon the same. It was this same fire that filled the temple of Solomon at the time of its dedication. It is this same fire that surrounds the Holy One of Israel: hence, Paul calls Him, "a consuming fire." It was this same fire which all who sincerely received John's baptism, had the promise of being baptized with. It was this same fire and Holy Ghost that descended from heaven like a rushing mighty wind, on the day of Pentecost—that was seen in the form of cloven tongues—that controlled the tongues of the disciples to speak in many languages unknown to themselves. (*Discourses on the Holy Ghost*, pp. 37–38.)

Brigham Young declared:

If we could see our heavenly Father, we should see a being similar to our earthly parent, with this difference, our Father in heaven is exalted and glorified. He has received His thrones, His principalities and powers, and He sits as a governor, as a monarch, and overrules kingdoms, thrones, and dominions that have been bequeathed to Him, and such as we anticipate receiving. While He was in the flesh, as we are, He was as we are. But it is now written of Him that our God is as a consuming fire, that He dwells in everlasting burnings, and this is why sin cannot be where He is.

There are principles that will endure through all eternity, and no fire can obliterate them from existence. They are those principles that are pure, and fire is made typical use of to show the glory and purity of the gods, and of all perfect beings. (*Journal of Discourses,* 4:54.)

Fire also served as a purifier and thus was a natural symbol for the Holy Ghost, who is the sanctifier. John the Baptist told those he immersed in the waters of Jordan that he baptized them unto repentance, but that one would come after him who was greater than he, one "whose shoes," he said, "I am not worthy to bear: he shall baptize you with the Holy Ghost, and with fire" (Matthew 3:11; Luke 3:16). Both the Book of Mormon and the Doctrine and Covenants repeatedly refer to those who have been baptized and have actually received the companionship of the Spirit as those who have received "the baptism of fire and of the Holy Ghost" (2 Nephi 31:13, 14; 3 Nephi 9:20; D&C 19:31; 20:41). That is, they have been purged of sin—the spiritual dross has been burned from their souls—and they have been purified, thus being worthy of companionship with the Holy Ghost. To such, as we have discussed, God grants priceless gifts of the Spirit, whose reception and use are inseparably connected with righteousness.

"The symbolism of receiving the gift of the Holy Ghost is that of lighting a perpetual flame within the soul, one which provides light and warmth while constantly purging that which is unclean from it. This is very different from the notion in the sectarian world that some supposed spiritual experience brings the assurance of salvation. That is more like being struck with lightning than the scriptural imagery of a flame that was to perpetually burn within the temple, fueled with works of righteousness." (Joseph Fielding McConkie, *Gospel Symbolism,* p. 197.)

Throughout the scriptures, fire is a symbol of spiritual power, illumination, inspiration, and enlightenment; it is also associated with testing. Writing to the Corinthians, Paul said: "Every man's work shall be made manifest; for the day shall declare it, because it shall be revealed by fire; and the fire shall try every man's work of what sort it is. If any man's work abide which he hath built thereupon, he shall receive a reward. If any man's work shall be burned, he shall suffer loss; but he himself may be saved; yet so as by fire." (JST, 1 Corinthians 3:13–15.) Paul is saying, in effect: Every man will be judged by his doctrine. If he has taught sound doctrine he will be richly rewarded. If, on the other hand, his doctrine has not been sound, though he himself was sincere and well-intentioned, his works of necessity will be burned. But he can repent of his errors and build anew. He is without reward, but not without the chance to correct that which was born of ignorance.

Paul's promise does not extend to those who, with malice and bitterness, oppose the truth. Those who fight the light of the gospel to protect the darkness that hides their own evil deeds need not suppose that such merciful treatment will be theirs in the day of judgment. Further, it must be understood that the fire mentioned here is that which tries a man's works, not that fire which purifies his soul. The doctrine herein espoused by Paul is illustrated by the role of the Holy Ghost as the Holy Spirit of Promise. As we have seen, only those doctrines and those works that are good can bear that seal which assures that they will be of "efficacy, virtue, or force in and after the resurrection from the dead" (D&C 132:7). Sincerity of purpose will not exalt a misdirected doctrine.

It is in this context that Paul inquires, "Know ye not that ye are the temple of God, and that the Spirit of God dwelleth in you?" He then declares: "If any man defile the temple of God, him shall God destroy: for the temple of God is holy, which temple ye are." (1 Corinthians 3:16–17.) In so saying, Paul affirms that as the earth was baptized by water in the days of Noah, so it must be baptized by fire at the time of the Second Coming, for no unclean thing can abide the presence of God (2 Thessalonians 1:7–9). "Every corruptible thing, both of man, or of the beasts of the field, or of the fowls of the heavens, or of the fish of the sea, that dwells upon all the face of the earth, shall be consumed; and also that of element shall melt with fervent heat; and all things shall become new, that my knowledge and glory may dwell upon all the earth" (D&C 101:24–25). As the soul of man must be sanctified, or purified, to enjoy association with that which is holy, so the earth must be, as well as all that are upon it.

Pure Olive Oil

"And then, at that day, before the Son of man comes, the kingdom of heaven shall be likened unto ten virgins, who took their lamps, and went forth to meet the bridegroom. And five of them were wise, and five of them were foolish. They that were foolish took their lamps and took no oil with them; but the wise took oil in their vessels with their lamps.'' (JST, Matthew 25:1-6.) So begins one of the best known of Jesus' parables. That we might not be numbered among the unwise virgins, the Savior himself has given those of our day an interpretation of it. ''At that day, when I shall come in my glory,'' he explained, ''shall the parable be fulfilled which I spake concerning the ten virgins. For they that are wise and have received the truth, and have taken the Holy Spirit for their guide, and have not been deceived—verily I say unto you, they shall not be hewn down and cast into the fire, but shall abide the day.'' (D&C 45:56-57.) Thus we learn that the oil by which the pure are to be guided to the marriage feast, or more particularly to those sacred covenants with the Master by which salvation comes, is the Holy Spirit.

It would be difficult to imagine a more perfect metaphor or simile for the Holy Ghost than pure olive oil. Among those of the ancient Near East, olive oil was a source of light, warmth, nourishment, and healing. ''Olive oil,'' wrote Truman G. Madsen, ''was used both internally and externally. It was a cooking oil, made better by heating, and was a condiment for salads and breads and meats. The pure oil had other vital uses: it was an almost universal antidote, reversing the effects of a variety of poisons. It was often used in a poultice believed to drain infection or sickness. As an ointment, olive oil—mingled with other liquids—soothed bruises and wounds and open sores.'' Further, ''the image of pouring oil on troubled waters, and the associated olive branch of peace—such as the offering of peace and relief to Noah after raging seas—were common in Bible lore. In other spiritual contexts oil was the token of forgiveness.'' (''The Olive Press,'' *Ensign*, December 1982, pp. 58-59.)

Anointing with Oil

Of the Savior, the scriptures declare that God ''hath highly exalted him, and given him a name which is above every name: that at the name of Jesus every knee should bow, of things in heaven, and things in earth, and things under the earth; and that every tongue should confess that Jesus Christ is Lord, to the glory of God the Father'' (Philippians 2:9–11). The name *Jesus* means ''Jehovah saves,'' and connotes the idea that salvation is in him. *Christ* is a title which means ''anointed'' or ''anointed one.'' In Old Testament times anointing was the principal and divinely appointed ceremony in the inauguration of prophets, priests, and kings. The anointing was a ritual consecration or setting apart to sacred purposes. The ritual centered in the pouring of pure olive oil upon the head of the one being anointed, in a symbolic representation of the Spirit of the Lord that was to be poured out upon him and, through him, upon the nation of Israel. Under the leadership of her prophets, priests, and kings, Israel was to walk in paths of righteousness, each prophet, priest, and king being a type or symbolic representation of the Christ who would be the great Prophet, Priest, and King.

All that we do for the salvation of men is to be done in the sacred name of Christ. It naturally follows that all that is properly done in the name of Christ is attended by an outpouring of the Spirit. The act of anointing the head with pure olive oil is but the symbolic manifestation of that spiritual outpouring. Thus John writes, ''Ye have an unction [anointing] from the Holy One, and ye know all things'' (1 John 2:20), or in the more perfect expression of Moroni, ''By the power of the Holy Ghost ye may know the truth of all things'' (Moroni 10:5).

''But the anointing which ye have received of him abideth in you,'' John continues, ''and ye need not that any man teach you: but as the same anointing teacheth you of all things, and is truth, and is no lie, and even as it hath taught you, ye shall abide in him'' (1 John 2:27). As illustration of this principle, we read that as Christ awaited the day of his ministry to come, ''he served under his father, and he spake not as other men, neither could he be taught; for he needed not that any man should teach him'' (JST, Matthew 3:25). It need not be supposed that Christ was not taught by his earthly guardians or by teachers as were other youth; rather we are to understand that he learned all gospel principles under the tutelage of the Holy Ghost.

Such is to be true of all who would declare his gospel in his name; the Holy Ghost must also be the source of that which they have been commissioned to teach. "Hearken ye elders of my church, whom I have appointed," came the voice of the Lord to those commissioned to teach the gospel in our dispensation. "Ye are not sent forth to be taught, but to teach the children of men the things which I have put into your hands by the power of my Spirit; and ye are to be taught from on high. Sanctify yourselves and ye shall be endowed with power, that ye may give even as I have spoken." (D&C 43:15-16.)

The endowment referred to in the above verse appropriately embraced a ritual washing and an anointing with oil, signifying the participant's desire to consecrate both mind and body to the Lord's service. In dedicating the Kirtland Temple, Joseph Smith prayed: "Let the anointing of thy ministers be sealed upon them with power from on high. Let it be fulfilled upon them, as upon those on the day of Pentecost; let the gift of tongues be poured out upon thy people, even cloven tongues as of fire, and the interpretation thereof. . . . Put upon thy servants the testimony of the covenant, that when they go out and proclaim thy word they may seal up the law." (D&C 109:35-38.)

The ordinance of administering to the sick is also associated with the anointing of oil. From the New Testament we learn that the missionaries of Christ's day "anointed with oil many that were sick, and healed them" (Mark 6:13). The sick person was instructed to call for "the elders of the church; and [to] let them pray over him, anointing him with oil in the name of the Lord." Then came the promise that "the prayer of faith shall save the sick, and the Lord shall raise him up; and if he have committed sins, they shall be forgiven him." (James 5:14-15.) Such has ever been the order among the household of faith (see D&C 42:44). As in other rituals that involve the outpouring of oil consecrated and dedicated for the blessing of the Saints, the ritual of administering to the sick also represents the needed outpouring of the Spirit.

Anciently, anointing was a token of prosperity and produced a spirit of cheerfulness (Psalm 104:15). Hence this spiritual unction is figuratively described as anointing "with the oil of gladness"

(Psalm 45:7; Hebrews 1:9) or the "oil of joy" (Isaiah 61:3). It is a perfect symbolic expression for the manifestation of the Spirit, the outpouring of the Holy Ghost.

A Rushing Mighty Wind

Whence comes the witness of the Spirit? In response to such a question, the Savior said: "The wind bloweth where it listeth, and thou hearest the sound thereof, but canst not tell whence it cometh, and whither it goeth: so is every one that is born of the Spirit" (John 3:8). We cannot see wind, but only its effects. It blows in a variety of directions—we hear its sounds, perceive its operations in the motion of trees, feel it push on our backs or sting our cheeks—but we cannot see it. So it is with the operations of the Spirit. We cannot see them, we cannot tell whence they come, and we know not where they will lead us; yet their effect upon us is most obvious. Indeed, in Hebrew the words *spirit* and *wind* are identical.

On the day of Pentecost, the Twelve were assembled in the upper room "and suddenly there came a sound from heaven as of a rushing mighty wind, and it filled all the house where they were sitting. And there appeared unto them cloven tongues like as of fire, and it sat upon each of them. And they were filled with the Holy Ghost, and began to speak with other tongues, as the Spirit gave them utterance." (Acts 2:2–4.) In the dedicatory prayer of the Kirtland Temple, the Prophet Joseph Smith pleaded for that same Spirit that attended the meridian day of Pentecost. "Let thy house be filled, as with a rushing mighty wind, with thy glory," he petitioned the heavens (D&C 109:37). His prayer did not go unheeded. We read: "Brother George A. Smith arose and began to prophesy, when a noise was heard like the sound of a rushing mighty wind, which filled the Temple, and all the congregation simultaneously arose, being moved upon by an invisible power; many began to speak in tongues and prophesy; others saw glorious visions; and I beheld the Temple was filled with angels, which fact I declared to the congregation. The people of the neighborhood came running together (hearing an unusual sound within, and seeing a bright light like a pillar of fire resting upon the Temple), and were astonished at what was taking place. This continued until the meeting closed at eleven p.m." (*History of the Church,* 2:428.)

Conclusion

Symbols help compensate for the inadequacy of words. They greatly expand our sense and feel of the nature, purpose, and manner in which the third member of the Godhead teaches and testifies of the verities of heaven. Thus the grace, peace, and gentleness of the Spirit is likened to a dove; and the whisperings of the Holy Ghost are likened to the blowing of the wind, which we feel but do not see, and whose all-consuming presence can warm our souls or even burn like fire within us. To the ancients, the Holy Ghost was the "oil of joy for mourning, the garment of praise for the spirit of heaviness" (Isaiah 61:3), and the "oil of gladness" for those who loved righteousness and hated wickedness (Psalm 45:7). It is the holy oil of anointing, the outpouring of the Spirit, by which one takes upon himself the name of Christ. "And again, I say unto you, all things must be done in the name of Christ, whatsoever you do in the Spirit" (D&C 46:31).

8

The Comforter

The Comforter, which is the Holy Ghost, whom the Father will send in my name, . . . shall teach you all things, and bring all things to your remembrance.
—John 14:26

While the Savior ministered among mortals, the Saints were able to rejoice in his love and bask in his light. Surely there was no more settled and secure feeling than to enjoy the companionship of the Creator of heaven and earth, as he dwelt in the flesh. And yet as his Galilean ministry drew to a close, he promised his devoted disciples that he would send another in his stead to assist them in his absence. "If ye love me," he said, "keep my commandments. And I will pray the Father, and he shall give you another Comforter, that he may abide with you for ever; even the Spirit of truth." (John 14:15-17.)

This was a gift that had been known by the ancients and was enjoyed by the primitive Saints. Indeed, no more descriptive word could be used to signify the work of the Holy Ghost than that of Comforter. This member of the Godhead is sent by the Father and the Son to bring comfort, to lift burdens, to ease pains, to strengthen in times of difficulty, and to teach the things of immortal glory. He is the helper, the healer, the advocate and messenger of the Father and the Son. And because "the Comforter knoweth all things" (D&C 42:17; 35:19), "he will guide [us] into all truth . . . and he will shew [us] things to come" (John 16:13).

The Comfort of Personal Purity

The greatest burden a man or woman can bear in this life is the burden of sin. Sin estranges. It alienates. If allowed to remain and thus not repented of it leads to hopelessness and despair (Moroni 10:22). And thus it is that one of the greatest comforts in this life is the assurance that one's sins have been remitted, that one has been forgiven. Stated President Harold B. Lee, "The greatest miracles I see today are not necessarily the healing of sick bodies, but . . . the healing of sick souls, those who are sick in soul and spirit and are downhearted and distraught" (Conference Report, April 1973, p. 178).

"Men are prepared for salvation," Oscar W. McConkie wrote, "through forgiveness of sins. And they are comforted when they are no longer under the bond of sin. The Holy Ghost comforts all who love God and are cleansed of sin. All others are comfortless." Continuing, he observed:

> The cumulative powers of the Father, Son, and Holy Ghost, straightway comfort all who receive them. But the Holy Ghost is especially ordained to comfort the faithful, and to give them assurance of the forgiveness of their transgressions. Because of Christ, the Father absolves the repentant from sin, knowledge of which is the most comforting of all knowledge. And the Holy Ghost expands their minds, stores truth in them, and preserves righteous purpose. The Son sees every sorrow in the righteous, and heals them, but he will not send the Holy Ghost to comfort any who gangrene their flesh with wickedness, or who invite any mortification of their strength. Thus, because of Christ, the repentant are washed clean by the Holy Ghost, which destroys all their fear, washes all evil out of them, and gives them assurance of salvation, which is the most comforting thing that God can do for them. (*The Holy Ghost,* pp. 61, 63.)

Though it is true that sins and iniquity are removed by the blood of Christ, through the precious blood of the "Lamb slain from the foundation of the world" (Revelation 13:8; Moses 7:47), the Holy Ghost is the agent, the means by which a remission of sins and the consequent comfort comes. Nephi called upon mankind to follow the example of their Lord and Master and enter the waters of baptism to fulfill the commandment of the Father. "Wherefore," he counseled, "do the things which I have told you I have seen that your Lord and your Redeemer should do; for, for this cause have they been shown unto me, that ye might know the gate by which ye should enter. For the gate by which ye should enter is repentance and baptism by water; *and then cometh a remission of your sins by fire and by the Holy Ghost.*" (2 Nephi 31:17, italics added.) Moroni explained that in the Church of Christ "none were received unto baptism save they took upon them the name of Christ, having a determination to serve him to the end. And after they had been received unto baptism, and *were wrought upon and cleansed by the power of the Holy Ghost,* they were numbered among the people of the church of Christ." (Moroni 6:3-4, italics added; compare 3 Nephi 12:2.)

There are two baptisms—the baptism of water and the baptism of fire and of the Holy Ghost. Both are required for a remission of sins; both are essential for salvation (see D&C 76:52). Water baptism alone will not cleanse the penitent, for it is absolutely necessary for filth and dross to be burned out of the soul by the fire of the Spirit. "You might as well baptize a bag of sand as a man," Joseph Smith explained, "if not done in view of the remission of sins and getting of the Holy Ghost. Baptism by water is but half a baptism, and is good for nothing without the other half—that is, the baptism of the Holy Ghost." (*Teachings of the Prophet Joseph Smith,* p. 314.) "Sins are remitted," Elder Bruce R. McConkie has written, "not in the waters of baptism, as we say in speaking figuratively, but when we receive the Holy Ghost. It is the Holy Spirit of God that erases carnality and brings us into a state of righteousness. We become clean when we actually receive the fellowship and companionship of the Holy Ghost. It is then that sin and dross and evil are burned out of our souls as though by fire. The baptism of the Holy Ghost is the baptism of fire." (*A New Witness for the Articles of Faith,* p. 290; see also p. 239.)

Mormon wrote of an experience of the people of King Benjamin and in so doing provided a pattern by which the Saints in all ages may know when their sins have been remitted. After Benjamin had given an account of his reign and ministry and called his people to the noble service of their fellow beings; after he had spoken the words delivered to him by an angel, had testified of the coming of the Lord Omnipotent to atone for the sins of the world; after he had taught with fervor and conviction that the natural man is an enemy of God and must be put off through godly sorrow and sincere repentance—the people after all this, now overwhelmed with the power and personal significance of the message, fell to the earth, "for the fear of the Lord had come upon them. And they had viewed themselves in their own carnal state, even less than the dust of the earth." Thereafter, "they all cried aloud with one voice, saying: O have mercy, and apply the atoning blood of Christ that we may receive forgiveness of our sins, and our hearts may be purified." After they had spoken these words, *"the Spirit of the Lord came upon them,* and they were filled with joy, *having received a remission of their sins,* and *having peace of conscience,* because of the exceeding faith which they had in Jesus Christ who should come." (Mosiah 4:1-3, italics added.)

When a person's sins have been forgiven, the painful memory of the offense begins to fade, as does the awful aloneness which follows in the wake of sin. The Holy Ghost cannot dwell in an unclean tabernacle (1 Corinthians 3:16-17; see also Alma 11:37; 3 Nephi 27:19). A person who begins once again to enjoy the influence and gifts of the Spirit—an influence which the Saints come to treasure and whose loss is painful and poignant—may rest assured that he or she is no longer unclean. The Comforter reproves for sin (John 16:8-11), removes the sin, and regenerates the sinner. Such a process leads to joy, to that "peace of conscience" associated with knowing that the Lord remembers the sin no more (D&C 58:42).

The Comfort of Perspective

The Holy Ghost as the third member of the Godhead possesses the attributes of God, and as such speaks and acts in behalf of the Father and the Son. To receive the word of the Spirit is to know the word of the Father. To gain the direction of the Spirit is to gain the mind of Christ. "This Spirit is perfect. Therefore, all that he does is perfect, hence his teachings are perfect. . . . [He] is unto men in place of God, instructing them according to the desires of the Father.'' (Oscar McConkie, *The Holy Ghost,* p. 76.) One of the roles of the Holy Ghost is to provide man with the perspective of God, the vision of things as they really are, the view of life and death from loftier heights.

''Life's starkest reality is death. Death is 'a subject which strikes dread—even terror—into the hearts of most men. It is something we fear, of which we are sorely afraid, and from which most of us would flee if we could.' . . . Life's bitter winters may find us walking alone. During these cold and dark seasons of solitude, we wrap ourselves in the protective clothing of faith and its perspective and are warmed by precious memories. Thus we move on, seeking always to view things as God views them.'' (Robert L. Millet and Joseph Fielding McConkie, *The Life Beyond,* pp. 14–15.) Perhaps at no time do we need and seek the comfort of the Spirit more than at the time of the loss of a loved one. Through the power of the Spirit, in time the pain of personal loss comes to be swallowed up in the realization that the loved one continues in another sphere of existence beyond the veil; that life and labor and love are eternal; and that reunion is a definite though delayed reality. ''Precious in the sight of the Lord,'' the Psalmist declares, ''is the death of his saints'' (Psalm 116:15). The ''peace . . . which passeth all understanding'' (Philippians 4:7) is beyond unillumined man's grasp, a peace which transcends mortal man's capacity to either comprehend or convey. It is of God.

Living in troubled and sinful times may lead some to despair. Others may conclude that little can be done to reform a reprobate world and may thereafter feel bitterness and animosity toward those who bring a stench and a stain upon humanity. Those Saints who seek the influence of the Comforter will, however, take a different course: they will come to view the world as the Lord does. An experience in the life of Alma the Younger will illustrate what often happens to those who open themselves to the Spirit's promptings.

Having witnessed the sham and hypocrisy and self-righteousness of the Zoramites as they made their way to the top of the Rameumptom and uttered their set prayer, Alma and his missionary companions were "astonished beyond all measure." When Alma had witnessed these things, "his heart was grieved; for he saw that they were a wicked and a perverse people." He then cried out to God in mighty prayer: "O, how long, O Lord, wilt thou suffer that thy servants shall dwell here below in the flesh, to behold such gross wickedness among the children of men? . . . O Lord God, how long wilt thou suffer that such wickedness and infidelity shall be among this people? O Lord," Alma then pleaded, "wilt thou give me strength, that I may bear with mine infirmities. For . . . such wickedness among this people doth pain my soul. O Lord," he continued—and notice now his petition to God—"my heart is exceedingly sorrowful; wilt thou comfort my soul in Christ." Alma then prayed fervently for that same comfort in behalf of his missionary companions. "O Lord," he asked, "wilt thou comfort their souls in Christ."

Alma's desire for the well-being of the Zoramites, however, overshadowed his abhorrence for their sins. He requested that the Lord grant him and his party success in converting the Zoramites. At this point we observe a marvelous transformation in his prayer —a transformation born of the Spirit: "Behold, O Lord, their souls are precious, and many of them are our brethren; therefore, give unto us, O Lord, power and wisdom that we may bring these, our brethren, again unto thee." (Alma 31:19–35.) "What a difference it would make," President Harold B. Lee taught, "if we really sensed our divine relationship to God, our Heavenly Father, our relationship to Jesus Christ, our Savior and our elder brother, and our relationship to each other" (Conference Report, October 1973, p. 9). Such is the understanding that comes to us by the power and through the gift of the Holy Ghost.

As Latter-day Saints, at one time or another all of us are challenged by questions, for instance, on matters pertaining to our history or our theology. In such instances we do well to utilize the powers of the Comforter—to gain that assurance and direction when questions may not yet be answered to our satisfaction, when doubts remain, and when difficult issues need to be placed on the shelf for a time. The witness of this work—the vitality and veracity of the Restoration—is fundamental and basic to one's peace. Such a witness can come to every member of the Church and can serve as an anchor in troubled waters. No one is expected to follow the lead of the Apostles and prophets blindly. All are encouraged and counseled to seek an unshakable faith; in doing so, they become more powerful advocates for the cause of truth.

But generally, the acquiring of such a testimony comes only in process of time. Saints who learn to deal wisely with their doubts move forward "in all patience and faith" (D&C 21:5), seeking always that quiet rest of the Spirit which results eventually in a settled conviction of the truth (see Joseph F. Smith, *Gospel Doctrine,* pp. 58, 126). In time the people of God come to know, by the power of the Holy Ghost, who they are, whose they are, and why they are. President Brigham Young taught:

> The Holy Ghost takes of the Father, and of the Son, and shows it to the disciples [see John 16:13–15]. It shows them things past, present, and to come. It opens the vision of the mind, unlocks the treasures of wisdom, and they begin to understand the things of God; . . . they comprehend themselves and the great object of their existence. They also comprehend the designs of the wicked one, and the designs of those who serve him; they comprehend the designs of the Almighty in forming the earth, and mankind upon it, and the ultimate purpose of all His creations. It leads them to drink at the fountain of eternal wisdom, justice, and truth; they grow in grace, and in knowledge of the truth as it is in Jesus Christ, until they see as they are seen and know as they are known. (*Journal of Discourses,* 1:241.)

The Comfort of Knowing the Peaceable Things

In a revelation given to Edward Partridge following his baptism, the Lord said: "I will lay my hand upon you by the hand of my servant Sidney Rigdon, and you shall receive my Spirit, the Holy Ghost, *even the Comforter, which shall teach you the peaceable things of the kingdom*" (D&C 36:2, italics added). To James Covill the word of Jehovah also came: "And verily, verily, I say unto you, he that receiveth my gospel receiveth me; and he that re-

ceiveth not my gospel receiveth not me. And this is my gospel—
repentance and baptism by water, and then cometh the baptism of
fire and the Holy Ghost, even *the Comforter, which showeth all
things, and teacheth the peaceable things of the kingdom.''* (D&C
39:5-6, italics added.)

The ''peaceable things of the kingdom'' are things in the realm
of the Spirit, matters which can only be known and understood by
revelation. They are the mysteries of God, those sacred verities
which are unknown to and unknowable by the wayward and the
worldly. They bring peace to the faithful and confusion to the
faithless. The peaceable things of the kingdom are the insights and
impressions which distill upon the souls of the righteous and bring
joy, those sacred perceptions which, on the other hand, are
relegated by the worldly wise or undiscerning to the realm of foolishness. ''If thou shalt ask,'' we have been promised, ''thou shalt
receive revelation upon revelation, knowledge upon knowledge,
that thou mayest know the mysteries and peaceable things—that
which bringeth joy, that which bringeth life eternal'' (D&C 42:61).
To receive the peaceable things of the kingdom is to receive the
witness of ''the record of heaven; the Comforter; the peaceable
things of immortal glory; the truth of all things; that which quick-
eneth all things, which maketh alive all things; that which knoweth
all things, and hath all power according to wisdom, mercy, truth,
justice, and judgment'' (Moses 6:61). To know the peaceable
things is to know the things of God.

To have the mind of the Lord is particularly important when we
pray. Proper prayer is addressed to the Father, in the name of the
Son, by the power of the Holy Ghost. ''Let us stop and ponder. We
are to pray in the name of Jesus Christ. What does it mean? Is it
not the same as with miracles and ordinances and prophesying and
preaching? All are done in his name. When we pray in Christ's
name, among other things, we put ourselves in his place and stead.
We say the words he would say, because our prayers, when they
meet the divine standard, are spoken by the power of the Holy
Ghost. And because they are spoken in the name of the Blessed
Jesus, our words become his words; they are what he would say in
the same situation.'' (Robert L. Millet and Joseph Fielding Mc-
Conkie, *In His Holy Name*, p. 56.)

Those who seek to purify their hearts before God; who avoid the very appearance of evil; who seek with all their might to rise above the carnal and the sensual; and who devote themselves to consistent and yearning prayer—such persons, on occasion, find their words reaching beyond their thoughts; they discover that the words of their petitions have been given to them from above. "He that asketh in the Spirit asketh according to the will of God; wherefore it is done even as he asketh" (D&C 46:30). "And if ye are purified and cleansed from all sin," the Lord said, "ye shall ask whatsoever you will in the name of Jesus and it shall be done. But know this, *it shall be given you what you shall ask.*" (D&C 50:29-30, italics added.) Paul taught that "the Spirit also helpeth our infirmities: for we know not what we should pray for as we ought: but the Spirit itself maketh intercession for us with [striving] which cannot be [expressed]. And he that searcheth the hearts [that is, Christ, who sends the Comforter] knoweth what is the mind of the Spirit, because he maketh intercession for the saints according to the will of God." (Romans 8:26-27; *Teachings of the Prophet Joseph Smith*, p. 278.) Indeed, the Holy Ghost teaches us not only that we should pray but *how* to pray and *what* to pray for (see 2 Nephi 32:8-9).

This, of course, is the key to having our prayers answered. Thus Christ could deliver the following transcendent promise to Nephi, son of Helaman: "And now, because thou hast [labored] with such unwearyingness, behold, I will bless thee forever; and I will make thee mighty in word and in deed, in faith and in works; yea, even that *all things shall be done unto thee according to thy word, for thou shalt not ask that which is contrary to my will*" (Helaman 10:5, italics added). When Jesus was among the Nephites in America, he commanded his Apostles to pray. "And it came to pass that . . . they did not multiply many words, for it was given unto them what they should pray, and they were filled with desire" (3 Nephi 19:24). Such prayer becomes more than petitionary—it becomes instructive and revelatory in scope; we learn things from what we speak. "When you have labored faithfully for years," Brigham Young explained, "you will learn this simple fact—that if your hearts are aright, and you still continue to be obedient, continue to serve God, continue to pray, the spirit of revelation will be in you like a well of water springing up to ever-lasting life" (*Journal of Discourses,* 12:103). Further, President Young counseled, "Let all persons be fervent in prayer, until they know the things of God for themselves" (*Journal of Discourses,* 9:150).

The Comfort of Hope and Perfect Love

Hope burns brightly in the hearts of the faithful. It is a virtue and an attribute of the godly. Those who know not God or his ways, when introduced to the truth by a servant of the Lord, begin their trek of faith with hope—they hope that what has been preached is so, that there is a Lord and a Redeemer, a divinely de-vised plan for the salvation of God's children. They receive the baptism of water and of the Spirit and grow in spiritual graces from one level to a higher. Their initial hope for a Savior and for deliver-ance from the alienation they had known fades into the past and is replaced with a new hope—the blessed hope that through Christ they may attain eternal life. "Man must hope," Moroni reminded us, "or he cannot receive an inheritance in the place" which the Lord has prepared for the obedient (Ether 12:32). "And what is it that ye shall hope for?" Moroni later asked. "Behold I say unto you that ye shall have hope through the atonement of Christ and the power of his resurrection, to be raised unto life eternal." (Moroni 7:41.) Such hope is fostered within the hearts and minds of the faithful and is born of the Spirit, the Comforter.

"The first fruits of repentance is baptism," Moroni taught, "and baptism cometh by faith unto the fulfilling the command-ments; and the fulfilling the commandments bringeth remission of sins; and the remission of sins bringeth meekness, and lowliness of heart; and because of meekness and lowliness of heart cometh the visitation of the Holy Ghost, *which Comforter filleth with hope and perfect love,* which love endureth by diligence unto prayer, until the end shall come, when all the saints shall dwell with God" (Moroni 8:25–26, italics added). Perfect love—charity, the pure love of Christ (Moroni 7:47)—comes to men and women as a gift of God from the Comforter. To possess charity is to be motivated by heavenly power, to be driven by a sublime spirit that knows no earthly counterpart. To be filled with charity, which gift of the Spirit comes through diligent prayer and sustained worthiness (Moroni 7:48), is to love purely, as Christ does, as well as to love Christ purely. It is a gift which helps to provide purpose, depth, and commitment in relationships, giving richer meaning to life.

Those who are possessed of charity serve with an eye single to the glory of God; they labor for the welfare of Zion (2 Nephi 26:30–31); are selfless in their service and eager to bear, believe, and endure all things for the cause of truth and the good of their fellows (see Moroni 7:45; 1 Corinthians 13:4–7). Those upon whom the Comforter bestows the gift of charity are grounded in that hope and that conviction which help them to weather the storms of adversity and temptation: they face affliction with maturity and with that increased vision which allows them to serve God at all hazards. "Many of us," Joseph Smith explained, "have gone at the command of the Lord in defiance of everything evil, and obtained blessings unspeakable, in consequence of which our names are sealed in the Lamb's book of life, for the Lord has spoken it." Then, in stressing the importance of enjoying in our lives that quality of love granted by the Comforter, the Prophet taught that "until we have perfect love we are liable to fall and when we have a testimony that our names are sealed in the Lamb's book of life we have perfect love and then it is impossible for false Christs to deceive us." (*Teachings of the Prophet Joseph Smith,* p. 9.) The Saints in all ages are thus instructed to clothe themselves in the bond of charity, "as with a mantle, which is the bond of perfectness and peace" (D&C 88:125; Colossians 3:14).

In short, the Comforter, who is the Holy Ghost, leads men to all truth and brings that quality of life—that happiness—which is the object and design of our existence (*Teachings of the Prophet Joseph Smith,* p. 255). One young elder spoke eloquently of the ministrations of the Spirit and of the comfort and peace and power which may be ours through this heavenly gift. "At a period of this elder's life," the account goes, "when he was making determined effort to overcome his weaknesses and perform certain duties required of him, being worried and troubled, he had an experience which he could scarcely class as a vision, or as a dream, though it occurred in his sleep in the quiet of the night.''

He thought he saw himself in a kneeling posture with his face turned heavenward as though engaged in prayer, when there gradually stole over him a feeling of calm contentment, an utter forgetfulness of trouble, and an obliviousness to mortal surroundings. This sense of satisfaction increased to one of joy until his soul was wrapped in exquisite happiness, such as he had never experienced before in his most favored hours.

There was borne in upon his mind, taking possession of and quickening his heart, a sense of supreme possession. It was as if every righteous desire were granted, every good thing wished for in life were given; there was a fulness of re- alization overwhelming in its nature.

It seemed that he was aglow throughout his entire body with a warmth that was heavenly. . . .

In quiet thought and contemplation over what had oc- curred to him, there came as the most logical and reasonable explanation of it, the conclusion that for a brief period he had been permitted to taste, through the power of the Holy Spirit, celestial happiness; and an explanation, to some ex- tent at least, was therein found of the scripture quoted that man cannot see nor hear, nor understand, the extent of God's blessings. (*Improvement Era*, June 1905, pp. 623–24.)

Conclusion

A loving Father has not required us to traverse the paths of mor- tality alone. He has provided a priceless gift—the companionship of the Holy Ghost, the Comforter. It is the Comforter which is "shed forth upon [men] for the revelation of Jesus Christ" (D&C 90:11); more specifically, it is "the Comforter, which manifesteth that Jesus was crucified by sinful men for the sins of the world" (D&C 21:9); it is the Comforter who "knoweth all things, and beareth record of the Father and of the Son'' (D&C 42:17). It is the Comforter who brings peace to the troubled and the bereaved, who provides sustenance and support for the brokenhearted and the feeble-kneed. It is the Comforter who provides an elevated vision, hope in times of trial, revelation and divine direction in life's critical moments. God be thanked for the work and ministry of the Holy Ghost, our Comforter.

9

The New Birth

All mankind . . . must be born again; yea, born of God, changed from their carnal and fallen state, to a state of righteousness, being redeemed of God, becoming his sons and daughters; and thus they become new creatures.

—Mosiah 27:25–26

Membership in the Lord's kingdom is not enough. Having our names on the records of the true Church will not secure a place for us in the mansions prepared by the Savior. Nor will acceptance of the ordinances of salvation alone guarantee one a throne beside Abraham, Isaac, and Jacob. The gospel of Jesus Christ—that gospel covenant which is new in that it has been revealed anew in our day, but which is everlasting in that it has been a part of the lives of the faithful from the Edenic day—is "the power of God unto salvation" (Romans 1:16); it is the renovating power by which men and women are renewed and changed, by which they rise above the fallen and carnal state and enter the realm of divine experience. The gospel has been restored to change people—to make of them new creatures, new creatures in Christ.

Seeing and Entering the Kingdom

One of the most insightful episodes in scripture involves a conversation between Jesus and Nicodemus. John records:

There was a man of the Pharisees, named Nicodemus, a ruler of the Jews:

The same came to Jesus by night, and said unto him, Rabbi, we know that thou art a teacher come from God: for no man can do these miracles that thou doest, except God be with him.

Jesus answered and said unto him, Verily, verily, I say unto thee, Except a man be born again, he cannot see the kingdom of God.

Nicodemus saith unto him, How can a man be born when he is old? can he enter the second time into his mother's womb, and be born?

Jesus answered, Verily, verily, I say unto thee, Except a man be born of water and of the Spirit, he cannot enter into the kingdom of God. (John 3:1-5.)

It is difficult to know the exact meaning of (and thus the motivation behind) some of the things Nicodemus says. As "the master teacher in Israel" (a more literal rendering of verse 10), Nicodemus would have been familiar with the doctrine of the new birth. Such an idea did not originate with Jesus in the first century; as we now know, it was taught to Adam in the earliest ages of the earth's history (see Moses 6:59-61) and would have been a vital part of the prophetic message in every gospel dispensation from Adam to Christ. Nicodemus knew the scriptures; as a trained Pharisee, he would have been an expert in the Old Testament and well aware of numerous passages which attested to this verity. Had not the Lord spoken through Ezekiel of such a spiritual renewal associated with Israel's ultimate gathering? "I will take you from among the heathen," Jehovah had declared, "and gather you out of all countries, and will bring you into your own land." And now Ezekiel's allusion to the two baptisms: "Then will I sprinkle clean water upon you, and ye shall be clean: from all your filthiness, and from all your idols, will I cleanse you. *A new heart also will I give you; and a new spirit will I put within you:* and I will take away the stony heart out of your flesh, and I will give you an heart of flesh. And I will put my spirit within you, and cause you to walk in my statutes, and ye shall keep my judgments, and do them." (Ezekiel 36:24-27, italics added; compare Jeremiah 31:31-34.)

In the Book of Jubilees, a source revered in that day, the Lord explains to Moses concerning the ultimate purification of the house of Israel. "After this"—after Israel has acknowledged her sins and the sins of her fathers—"they will return to me in all uprighteousness and with all of their heart and soul. And I shall cut off the foreskin of their heart and the foreskin of the heart of their descendants. *And I shall create for them a holy spirit, and I shall purify them* so that they will not turn away from following me from that day and forever. And their souls will cleave to me and to all my commandments. And they will do my commandments. And I shall be a father to them, and they will be sons to me. And they will all be called 'sons of the living God.' . . . And I shall love them." (Jubilees 1:23–25, italics added, in Charlesworth, *The Old Testament Pseudepigrapha,* 2:54.)

"Nicodemus unwittingly but clearly revealed the fact that he did not know who Jesus was," President Marion G. Romney explained. "All he could see in the Son of God was a great teacher. This was all he could be expected to see, however, because he based his knowledge of who Jesus was upon what he had seen and heard of the Master's miracles. Perceiving this, Jesus informed him that the knowledge of divine things could not be had through man's normal senses." (Conference Report, October 1981, pp. 18–19.) Jesus was calling Nicodemus to a higher plane; he was extending the invitation to receive those ordinances and that Spirit which would allow him to see with spiritual eyes.

"It is one thing," Joseph Smith taught, "to *see* the kingdom of God, and another thing to *enter* into it. We must have a change of heart to see the kingdom of God, and subscribe [to] the articles of adoption to enter therein." (*Teachings of the Prophet Joseph Smith,* p. 328, italics added.) To have a change of heart is to have a change of mind, a change of vision, a change of perspective. To have a change of heart is to become aware of things which are ever-present but seldom witnessed. It is to awaken from the slumber of mediocrity, to shake off the effects of the sedative of insensitivity— to become alive to unseen realities. For Nicodemus or for any other person to *see* the kingdom of God is to begin the process of true conversion. Indeed, "one is converted when he sees with his eyes what he ought to see; when he hears with his ears what he ought to hear; and when he understands with his heart what he ought to understand. And what he ought to see, hear, and understand is truth—eternal truth—and then practice it. That is conversion." (Harold B. Lee, *Stand Ye in Holy Places*, p. 92.) President David O. McKay pointed out that Jesus "told Nicodemus that before he could solve the question that was troubling his mind, his spiritual vision would have to be changed by an entire revolution of his 'inner man.' His manner of thinking, feeling, and acting with reference to spiritual things would have to undergo a fundamental and permanent change with reference to spiritual matters. It is easy to see temporal things. It is easy to yield to lascivious things. It requires little or no effort to indulge in anything physical and animal-like. But to be born out of that world into a spiritual world is advancement that the Lord requires of each of us." (Conference Report, April 1960, p. 26.)

Daniel Tyler, an associate of the Prophet Joseph Smith, described the latter's teachings on seeing and entering the kingdom as follows:

> The birth here spoken of [John 3] . . . was not the gift of the Holy Ghost, which was promised after baptism, but was a portion of the Spirit, which attended the preaching of the gospel by the elders of the Church. The people wondered why they had not previously understood the plain declarations of scripture, as explained by the elders, as they had read them hundreds of times. When they read the Bible [now] it was a new book to them. This was being born again to see the kingdom of God. They were not in it, but could see it from the outside, which they could not do until the Spirit of the Lord took the veil from their eyes. It was a change of heart, but not of state; they were converted, but were yet in their sins. Although Cornelius [Acts 10] had seen an holy angel, and on the preaching of Peter the Holy Ghost was poured out upon him and his household, they were only born again to *see* the kingdom of God. Had they not been baptized afterwards they would not have been saved. (Cited in *Juvenile Instructor* 27 [1 February 1892]:93–94.)

To paraphrase the Prophet, to be born again to *see* is to gain a new vision—to recognize and acknowledge the kingdom of God and attend to the words of the Lord's servants who speak in his stead. As an example, one is born again when he "sees the power of God resting upon the leaders of this church, and [that testimony] goes down into his heart like fire." (Harold B. Lee, *Stand Ye in Holy Places*, p. 63.) To enter that kingdom one must subscribe to the articles of adoption—the first principles and ordinances of the gospel, the articles and statutes by which people are adopted into the family of Christ.

"Mere compliance with the formality of the ordinance of baptism," Elder McConkie has written, "does not mean that a person has been born again. No one can be born again without baptism, but the immersion in water and the laying on of hands to confer the Holy Ghost do not of themselves guarantee that a person has been or will be born again. The new birth takes place only for those who actually enjoy the gift of companionship of the Holy Ghost." (*Mormon Doctrine*, p. 101.) On the other hand, as the Prophet explained, a personal spiritual experience is not sufficient to bring about the new birth; equally essential are those rites and ordinances of the priesthood which prove to be the channel for the powers of godliness (D&C 84:20). Thus, "being born again, comes by the Spirit of God through ordinances" (*Teachings of the Prophet Joseph Smith*, p. 162).

Jesus' instruction to Nicodemus continued: "That which is born of the flesh is flesh," he said; "and that which is born of the Spirit is spirit. Marvel not that I said unto thee, Ye must be born again. The wind bloweth where it listeth, and thou hearest the sound thereof, but canst not tell whence it cometh, and whither it goeth: so is every one that is born of the Spirit." (John 3:6-8.) Nicodemus has been commanded by the Lord of life to be born again. The Greek word *anathen* may be translated as "again," or it may be rendered as "from above." The Pharisee is invited to be born "again," to breathe the breath of spiritual life, even as he had breathed the breath of life as a babe decades earlier. He is invited to be born "from above," to produce the fruits of heaven, to bring forth the works which characterize a son of God—"love, joy, peace, longsuffering, gentleness, goodness, faith, meekness, temperance" (Galatians 5:22). That person who is born of the Spirit is spiritual—he now lives as pertaining to righteousness, for he has died as pertaining to the ways of the worldly. He has crucified the old man of sin and come forth into a newness of life (Romans 6:3–6). Though he is not perfect, he does not continue in sinful ways (see JST, 1 John 3:6–9). That person who is "born of the flesh"—has joined the family of the faithless, and is thus begotten from beneath—is fleshly, brings forth the works of the flesh: "adultery, fornication, uncleanness, lasciviousness, idolatry, witchcraft, hatred, . . . wrath, strife, seditions, heresies, envyings, murders, drunkenness, revellings, and such like" (Galatians 5:19–21).

The Savior chose words for his instructions that were pertinent and appropriate. "The wind bloweth where it listeth," he said, "and thou hearest the sound thereof, but canst not tell whence it cometh, and whither it goeth: so is every one that is born of the Spirit" (John 3:8). Both the Hebrew word (*ruah*) and the Greek word (*pneuma*) which are translated as "wind" may be rendered as "breath" or "spirit." The word *sound* might also be rendered as "voice."

Man can neither predict nor program the Spirit of the Lord. To suggest that a sequence of deeds or performances will always result in an unusual outpouring of the Spirit, or to teach that spiritual gifts may be had through following a carefully constructed list of steps, may be misleading. The Lord knows best our spiritual bearing capacity, knows best all of those variables and circumstances which are beyond our grasp, and is thus able to decide perfectly what measure of spiritual experience we should receive. Although he grants to the children of men according to their desires and their works, he does so "in his own time, and in his own way, and according to his own will" (D&C 88:68). We simply cannot force spiritual things. Further, we cannot restrain the Spirit from determining the times of its comings and goings. "The presentation or 'gift' of the Holy Ghost," President Joseph F. Smith explained, "simply confers upon a man the right to receive at any time, when he is worthy of it and desires it, the power and light of truth of the Holy Ghost, although he may often be left to his own spirit and judgment." That is to say, the Holy Ghost "may be conferred upon men, and he may dwell with them for a while, or he may continue to dwell with them in accordance with their worthiness, and he may depart from them at his will." (*Gospel Doctrine*, pp. 60–61, 466; see also D&C 130:23.)

A Quickening in the Inner Man

In describing the spiritual renewal of father Adam in the opening dispensation of this world's history, Moses wrote: "And it came to pass, when the Lord had spoken with Adam, our father, that Adam cried unto the Lord, and he was caught away by the Spirit of the Lord, and was carried down into the water, and was laid under the water, and was brought forth out of the water. And thus he was baptized, and the Spirit of God descended upon him, *and thus he was born of the Spirit, and became quickened in the inner man.* And he heard a voice out of heaven, saying: Thou art baptized with fire, and with the Holy Ghost. This is the record of the Father, and the Son, from henceforth and forever." (Moses 6:64–66, italics added.) To quicken is to make alive, to animate, to energize. To be born again is to be quickened as pertaining to spiritual things.

To be born again is to gain heightened sensitivity to things that matter. For example, since much of the time the Holy Ghost works with members of the Church through their consciences, to be born again is to gain a deeper sensitivity to right and wrong, to enjoy greater manifestations of the gift of discernment, to develop more refined and educated desires. Since, as we shall see shortly, being born again consists in being adopted into the royal family and thus gaining godly attributes and qualities, experiencing the new birth entails feeling a deeper compassion and empathy for those who mourn or suffer or reach out for succor. The quickening in the inner man peels away the film and facade of sin, makes unnecessary the rigors and taxing labors of ostentation and superfluity; those who are born again see things clearly and sharply and are able to sift and sort out the sordid or even the tangential or the unimportant. They have less inclination to labor in secondary causes and a consuming but patient passion to occupy themselves in that which brings light and life and love. They come to treasure the simple pleasures in life and rejoice in the goodness of their God. Joseph Smith taught: "God has created man with a mind capable of instruction, and a faculty which may be enlarged in proportion to the heed and diligence given to the light communicated from heaven to the intellect; and that *the nearer man approaches perfection, the clearer are his views, and the greater his enjoyments, till he has overcome the evils of his life and lost every desire for sin;* and like the ancients, arrives at that point of faith where he is wrapped in the power and glory of his Maker and is caught up to dwell with Him." (*Teachings of the Prophet Joseph Smith,* p. 51, italics added.)

One who has been cleansed by the power of the Holy Ghost has his eyes opened, his spiritual eyes, to see and understand things neither apparent nor appealing to the natural man. Since "the natural man is an enemy to God" (Mosiah 3:19), since "all men that are in a state of nature" are "without God in the world" and are thereby in a state "contrary to the nature of happiness" (Alma 41:11), it follows that "[carnal] eye hath not seen, nor [fallen] ear heard, neither have entered into the heart of [unillumined] man, the things which God hath prepared for them that love him" (1 Corinthians 2:9).

In exulting with his brethren upon the tender mercies of God, Ammon first reminded them of their nefarious labors as persecutors of the Church. "Oh then," he said, "why did [the Lord] not consign us to an awful destruction, yea, why did he not let the sword of his justice fall upon us, and doom us to eternal despair?" Yet, Ammon noted, the great Jehovah did not condemn them nor destroy them but rather "in his great mercy hath brought us over that everlasting gulf of death and misery, even to the salvation of our souls." And then Ammon made a marvelous observation: "And now behold, my brethren," he continued, *"what natural man is there that knoweth these things? I say unto you, there is none that knoweth these things, save it be the penitent. Yea, he that repenteth and exerciseth faith, and bringeth forth good works, and prayeth continually without ceasing—unto such it is given to know the mysteries of God."* (Alma 26:19–22, italics added; compare Alma 36:4–5.) In speaking of the power of the Holy Ghost to bring about a quickening of the inner man, President

John Taylor explained that the operation of the Holy Ghost "is not something that affects the outward ear alone; it is not something that affects simply his judgment, but it affects his inner man; it affects the spirit that dwells within him; it is a part of God imparted unto man, if you please, giving him an assurance that God lives" (*Journal of Discourses,* 11:23).

President Harold B. Lee was fond of quoting Cyprian, the great defender of the faith after the apostolic period, concerning how a knowledge of spiritual realities comes. "Into my heart," Cyprian is reported to have said, "purified of all sin, there entered a light which came from on high and then suddenly, and in a marvelous manner, I saw certainty succeed doubt." (Cited in *Stand Ye in Holy Places,* p. 57; see also pp. 109, 354.) Those who are born again come to gain a conviction of their Lord and of this latter-day work which proves to be an anchor to their souls. In this sense they come to know things which no man can teach them (see Matthew 16:17; 1 John 2:27). President Marion G. Romney explained that his wife

> was reared in a home where they had prayer night and morning; where, almost daily, they discussed gospel principles around the family hearth. . . . In her struggle for an education, she developed an attitude of awe toward people who had been through college. As a member of a stake Sunday School board in Idaho Falls, she taught a class. There came to the class a nonmember of the Church, the wife of one of the brethren on the board. This woman had received a college degree from the University of Idaho. My wife, having not yet received her degree, was a little timid in the presence of this woman.
>
> One of the lessons in the course dealt with the First Vision of the Prophet Joseph Smith. As she made her preparation for the lesson, there came into her mind the realization that this nonmember would be present in the class. This realization was followed by the question, "What will she think of me, an ignorant girl, saying that the Father and the Son actually came down from heaven and appeared before a fourteen-year-old boy?" The thought terrified her, and she con-

cluded that she couldn't do it. She went to her mother, crying, and said, "Mother, I can't teach this lesson. I don't know that Joseph Smith saw the Father and the Son. I know I have been taught it all through my life by you and Father. I have believed you, but personally I don't know it. This woman will ridicule me. I just can't stand up before the class with this woman present and teach this lesson."

Now, her mother had not been to school very much. She was not an educated person by the world's standards, but she had faith in God the Eternal Father and in Jesus Christ, his Son, and she said to her daughter, "What did Joseph Smith do to get that vision?"

"Well," she answered, "he prayed."

"Why don't you do that?" she said to her daughter.

This young girl returned to her room and there, for the first time in her life in fact, she went to the Almighty with a sincere desire to know whether he lived and whether he and the Savior actually appeared to the Prophet Joseph. Coming out of that room, she went to her Sunday School class and taught that lesson with joy, with knowledge, with conviction. She had been born of the Spirit. She knew. (Conference Report, October 1981, pp. 19–21.)

President Lorenzo Snow has left us a description of what must surely be one of the most beautiful experiences of this dispensation pertaining to the new birth.

Some two or three weeks after I was baptized, one day while engaged in my studies, I began to reflect upon the fact that I had not obtained a *knowledge* of the truth of the work —that I had not realized the fulfillment of the promise [that] "he that doeth my will shall know of the doctrine," and I began to feel very uneasy. I laid aside my books, left the house, and wandered around through the fields under the oppressive influence of a gloomy, disconsolate spirit, while an indescribable cloud of darkness seemed to envelop me. I had been accustomed, at the close of the day, to retire for secret prayer, to a grove a short distance from my lodgings, but at this time I felt no inclination to do so. The spirit of prayer had departed and the heavens seemed like brass over my head. At length, realizing that the usual time had come for secret prayer, I concluded I would not forego my evening service, and, as a matter of formality, knelt as I was in the habit of doing, and in my accustomed retired place, but not feeling as I was wont to feel.

I had no sooner opened my lips in an effort to pray, than I heard a sound, just above my head, like the rustling of silken robes, and immediately the Spirit of God descended upon me, completely enveloping my whole person, filling me, from the crown of my head to the soles of my feet, and Oh, the joy and happiness I felt! No language can describe the almost instantaneous transition from a dense cloud of mental and spiritual darkness into a refulgence of light and knowledge . . . that God lives, that Jesus Christ is the Son of God, and of the restoration of the holy Priesthood, and the fulness of the Gospel. It was a complete baptism—a tangible immersion in the heavenly principle or element, the Holy Ghost; and even more real and physical in its effects upon every part of my system than the immersion by water; dispelling forever, so long as reason and memory last, all possibility of doubt or fear. . . .

I cannot tell how long I remained in the full flow of the blissful enjoyment and divine enlightenment, but it was several minutes before the celestial element which filled and surrounded me began gradually to withdraw. On arising from my kneeling posture, with my heart swelling with gratitude to God, beyond the power of expression, I felt—I *knew* —that He had conferred upon me what only an omnipotent being can confer—that which is of greater value than all the wealth and honors worlds can bestow. That night, as I retired to rest, the same wonderful manifestations were repeated, and continued to be for several successive nights. The sweet remembrance of those glorious experiences, from that time to the present, bring them fresh before me, imparting an inspiring influence which pervades my whole being, and I trust will to the close of my earthly existence. (Eliza R. Snow, *Biography and Family Record of Lorenzo Snow,* pp. 7-9.)

This experience of the young Lorenzo Snow, like that of the youthful Alma, is more dramatic than that experienced by the generality of faithful Saints, though the pattern is the same. Truly, "the Spirit giveth life" (2 Corinthians 3:6).

In speaking of the renovating power of Christ to make of men and women new creatures, President Ezra Taft Benson reminded the Saints that "the Lord works from the inside out. The world works from the outside in. The world would take people out of the slums. Christ takes the slums out of people, and then they take themselves out of the slums. The world would mold men by changing their environment. Christ changes men, who then change their environment. The world would shape human behavior, but Christ can change human nature." President Benson then pointed out that "Christ changes men, and changed men can change the world. Men changed for Christ will be captained by Christ. . . . Men captained by Christ will be consumed in Christ." (Conference Report, October 1985, pp. 5–6.) Being born again comes not simply as a result of a new way of thinking; it is far more than a shift in one's mental pattern. It comes by the blood of Christ through the transforming medium of the Holy Ghost. It is a change which is beyond the reach of man—even charismatic and capable man—to perform; it is a change that is of God, not man.

President David O. McKay shared a sacred experience, a story which illustrates the sobering responsiblity we have to be born again. In the midst of a world tour, he was approaching Apia, Samoa:

> I then fell asleep, and beheld in vision something infinitely sublime. In the distance I beheld a beautiful white city. Though far away, yet I seemed to realize that trees with luscious fruit, shrubbery with gorgeously-tinted leaves, and flowers in perfect bloom abounded everywhere. The clear sky above seemed to reflect these beautiful shades of color. I then saw a great concourse of people approaching the city. Each one wore a white flowing robe, and a white headdress. Instantly my attention seemed centered upon their Leader, and though I could see only the profile of his features and his body, I recognized him at once as my Savior! The tint

and radiance of his countenance were glorious to behold! There was a peace about him which seemed sublime—it was divine!

The city, I understood, was his. It was the City Eternal; and the people following him were to abide there in peace and eternal happiness.

But who were they?

As if the Savior read my thoughts, he answered by pointing to a semicircle that then appeared above them, and on which were written in gold the words: *"These Are They Who Have Overcome The World—Who Have Truly Been Born Again!"*

When I awoke, it was breaking day over Apia harbor. (*Cherished Experiences*, p. 6.)

Indeed, "when we awake and are born of God, a new day will break and Zion will be redeemed." (Ezra Taft Benson, Conference Report, October 1985, p. 6.)

In Process of Time

The Apostle Paul wrote to his beloved Saints in Rome, "now is our salvation nearer than when we believed" (Romans 13:11). Gaining salvation is a process; gaining the assurance that one will possess and receive and inherit the fulness of the glory of the Father is a lifelong process. And as it is with gaining salvation, so it is in regard to being born again. Though the new birth is a result of a definite time of decision—a desire for the things of righteousness —it is usually a quiet but steady process. Further, even though the change in one's nature may, in process of time, prove to be both definite and dramatic, it need not be accomplished instantaneously in order to be of God.

"Must there always be a visible, spiritual manifestation before one might be said to be born of the Spirit?" President Harold B. Lee asked. He then quoted passages from the Book of Mormon which tell of Alma's conversion (Mosiah 27:24-26; Alma 36:20-24), as well as verses suggesting the certain nature of change inherent in the new birth (Alma 5:14, 21), and added: "There are some of us who think that that same kind of experience has to be experienced by everybody, or he can't be saved. I once ran into a very serious situation where one of our teachers had inflamed some women, in a class he was teaching, until they almost had the kind of feeling that they had to have some kind of demonstration or else they hadn't been born of the Spirit." And then, after reading a portion of the experience of Lorenzo Snow (quoted earlier in this chapter), President Lee added: "Now, I repeat, because of some of these dramatic experiences, some of our teachers jump to the conclusion that one isn't born of the Spirit until he has had some such dramatic experience." (*Stand Ye in Holy Places,* pp. 58–60; see also *Times and Seasons,* 3:823.)

In speaking to a group of Brigham Young University students, Elder Bruce R. McConkie explained that "a person may get converted in a moment, miraculously. That is what happened to Alma the Younger. He had been baptized in his youth, he had been promised the Holy Ghost, but he had never received it. He was too worldly-wise. . . . In his instance the conversion was miraculous, in the snap of a finger, almost. . . . But that is not the way it happens with most people. With most people conversion is a process." (Address delivered at BYU First Stake Conference, 11 February 1968.) On another occasion he added:

> We say that a man has to be born again, meaning that he has to die as pertaining to the unrighteous things in the world. Paul said, "Crucify the old man of sin and come forth in a newness of life" (Romans 6:6). We are born again when we die as pertaining to unrighteousness and when we live as pertaining to the things of the Spirit. But *that doesn't happen in an instant, suddenly.* That . . . is a process. *Being born again is a gradual thing, except in a few isolated instances that are so miraculous that they get written up in the scriptures.* As far as the generality of the members of the Church are concerned, we are born again by degrees, and we are born again to added light and added knowledge and added desires for righteousness as we keep the commandments. ("Jesus Christ and Him Crucified," *1976 Devotional Speeches of the Year,* p. 399, italics added.)

Thus the Saints press forward with patient maturity and stead-fastness to keep the commandments, all the while praying for the cleansing and directing powers of the Spirit, but trusting in the Lord and his timetable.

Conclusion

The Holy Ghost is the midwife of salvation. He is the agent of the new birth, the sacred channel and power by which men and women are changed and renewed, made into new creatures. This new birth, which comes in process of time, brings membership in the family of God: such persons are redeemed from the Fall, reconciled to the Father through the Son, and made worthy of the designation of sons and daughters of Jesus Christ. (See Mosiah 5:1–7; 27:24–26; see also Robert L. Millet and Joseph Fielding McConkie, *In His Holy Name*, pp. 16–22.) They come to see and feel and understand things which the spiritually lifeless can never know. They become participants in the realm of divine experience.

10

Sanctified by the Spirit

*This is the commandment: Repent, all ye ends of the
earth, and come unto me and be baptized in my
name, that ye may be sanctified by the reception of
the Holy Ghost, that ye may stand spotless before me
at the last day.*

—3 Nephi 27:20

No unclean thing can dwell in the divine presence. The ultimate
object of the plan of salvation is to prepare men and women to be
with God. And thus it is that God has provided a means, a cleansing power from the effects of sin, a process by which the children of
the Father are renewed and readied and prepared for his presence.
Through the blood of Jesus Christ and by the power of the Holy
Ghost members of the Lord's Church are purified from sin and
made free from its damning effects. This process is known as sanctification.

Remitting Sin and Removing Sinfulness

At the time of the organization of the restored Church, the
Prophet Joseph Smith recorded: "We know that justification
through the grace of our Lord and Savior Jesus Christ is just and
true; and we know also, that sanctification through the grace of our
Lord and Savior Jesus Christ is just and true, to all those who love
and serve God with all their mights, minds, and strength" (D&C
20:30–31). To be *justified* is to be acquitted, to be made innocent,

to be exonerated. In the spiritual sense, to be justified is to be pronounced clean and free from sin.

Persons outside the Church who receive the message of the Restoration, repent of their sins, and are baptized by water and then by fire and the Holy Ghost are justified. Those within the covenant gospel repent of their sins, partake of the sacrament of the Lord's Supper, and seek to walk in paths of righteousness thereafter. The former have *obtained* a remission of sins and are thereby justified. The latter—citizens of the kingdom—are able to *retain* a remission of sins from day to day through acknowledging the goodness and graces of God; through magnifying their callings, and through offering their time and energies in selfless service to their fellowmen (see D&C 84:33; Mosiah 4:12, 26; Alma 4:13–14).

Finally, there is an ultimate sense in which one is justified in that his life is sealed, ratified, and approved by the Holy Spirit of Promise, the Holy Ghost. Our revelations thus speak of the candidates for celestial glory as those who "overcome by faith, and are sealed by the Holy Spirit of promise, which the Father sheds forth *upon all those who are just* and true." Such persons are "just men made perfect through Jesus the mediator of the new covenant, who wrought out this perfect atonement through the shedding of his own blood." (D&C 76:53, 69, italics added.) We shall speak more of the sealing role of the Holy Ghost in chapter 11.

Therefore "to be justified is to be free from sin, to be legally right before God. To be sanctified is to be free from the *effects* of sin, to have had sinfulness and the enticements of sin rooted out of our hearts and desires. To be sanctified in regard to vice is to shudder and shake at its appearance, to feel a revulsion for whatever allurements would detour or detain the human heart." (Robert L. Millet, *By Grace Are We Saved*, pp. 54–55.) Elder Orson Hyde explained that sanctification "means a purification of, or a putting away from, us, as individuals, and as a community, everything that is evil, or that is not in accordance with the mind and will of our heavenly Father." Further, Elder Hyde observed, sanctification is essential in our labors in the kingdom; such a process has "an eye to our own preservation for usefulness—for executing, carrying forward, and perpetuating the work of the Most High God." (*Journal of Discourses*, 1:71.)

The Holy Ghost is the sanctifier. He is the means whereby human hearts are made pure before God, whereby dross and iniquity are burned out of the soul as though by fire. In speaking of a group of ancient Saints who had received the holy priesthood and been cleansed by the blood of Christ and the sanctifying powers of the Spirit, Alma said:

> Now, as I said concerning the holy order, or this high priesthood, there were many who were ordained and became high priests of God; and it was on account of their exceeding faith and repentance, and their righteousness before God, they choosing to repent and work righteousness rather than to perish;
>
> Therefore they were called after this holy order, and were sanctified, and their garments were washed white through the blood of the Lamb.
>
> Now they, *after being sanctified by the Holy Ghost,* having their garments made white, being pure and spotless before God, could not look upon sin save it were with abhorrence; and there were many, exceedingly great many, who were made pure and entered into the rest of the Lord their God. (Alma 13:10–12, italics added; see also 5:54.)

The resurrected Lord likewise spoke of the central role of the Holy Ghost as the sanctifier in the gospel plan:

> And no unclean thing can enter into his kingdom; therefore nothing entereth into his rest save it be those who have washed their garments in my blood, because of their faith, and the repentance of all their sins, and their faithfulness unto the end.
>
> Now this is the commandment: Repent, all ye ends of the earth, and come unto me and be baptized in my name, *that ye may be sanctified by the reception of the Holy Ghost,* that ye may stand spotless before me at the last day.
>
> Verily, verily, I say unto you, this is my gospel; and ye know the things that ye must do in my church; for the works which ye have seen me do that shall ye also do; for that which ye have seen me do even that shall ye do. (3 Nephi 27:19–21, italics added.)

"After you have been immersed . . . in the water," Elder Orson Pratt taught, "and been cleansed and received the remission of your sins, you also have the promise of baptism of fire and of the Holy Ghost, by which you are . . . sanctified from all your evil affections, and you feel to love God and that which is just and true, and to hate that which is sinful and evil. Why? Because of this sanctifying, purifying principle that comes upon you, by the baptism of fire and the Holy Ghost." (*Journal of Discourses,* 16:319.) Elder B. H. Roberts insightfully observed:

Through water baptism is obtained a remission of past sins; but even after the sins of the past are forgiven, the one so pardoned will doubtless feel the force of sinful habits bearing heavily upon him. He who has been guilty of habitual untruthfulness, will at times find himself inclined, perhaps, to yield to that habit. He who has stolen may be sorely tempted, when opportunity arises, to steal again. While he who has indulged in licentious practices may again find himself disposed to give way to the seductive influence of the siren. So with drunkenness, malice, envy, covetousness, hatred, anger, and in short all the evil dispositions that flesh is heir to.

There is an absolute necessity for some additional sanctifying grace that will strengthen poor human nature, not only to enable it to resist temptation, but also to root out from the heart concupiscence—the blind tendency or inclination to evil. The heart must be purified, every passion, every propensity made submissive to the will, and the will of man brought into subjection to the will of God.

Man's natural powers are unequal to this task; so, I believe, all will testify who have made the experiment. Mankind stand in some need of a strength superior to any they possess of themselves, to accomplish this work of rendering pure our fallen nature. Such strength, such power, such a sanctifying grace is conferred on man in being born of the Spirit—in receiving the Holy Ghost. Such, in the main, is its office, its work. (*The Gospel and Man's Relationship to Deity,* pp. 169-70.)

To be sanctified is to be cleansed from sin's pulls and taunts, to be pure within and upright without. It is to desire and enjoy "truth in the inward parts." It is to be possessed of the wisdom of holiness.

Those of the household of faith who devote themselves to their duties, who perform with fidelity and devotion their assigned tasks and thus magnify their callings, are "sanctified by the Spirit unto the renewing of their bodies" (D&C 84:33). The Holy Ghost

> quickens all the intellectual faculties, increases, enlarges, expands, and purifies all the natural passions and affections, and adapts them, by the gift of wisdom, to their lawful use. It inspires, develops, cultivates, and matures all the fine-toned sympathies, joys, tastes, kindred feelings, and affections of our nature. It inspires virtue, kindness, goodness, tenderness, gentleness, and charity. It develops beauty of person, form, and features. It tends to health, vigor, animation, and social feeling. It invigorates all the faculties of the physical and intellectual man. It strengthens and gives tone to the nerves. In short, it is, as it were, marrow to the bone, joy to the heart, light to the eyes, music to the ears, and life to the whole being. (Parley P. Pratt, *Key to the Science of Theology*, p. 61.)

When men and women go to with their might to build up the kingdom of God and establish its righteousness, the Holy Ghost takes up an abode with them; he dwells with them and begins the process of sanctifying their souls.

When the Saints of the Most High labor not for gain or personal prominence but for Zion (2 Nephi 26:30–31), then they enjoy the ratifying stamp of approval of the sanctifier. In describing a group of steadfast Nephites who lived some forty years before Christ, Mormon wrote that "they did fast and pray oft, and did wax stronger and stronger in their humility, and firmer and firmer in the faith of Christ, unto the filling their souls with joy and consolation, yea, even to the purifying and the sanctification of their hearts, *which sanctification cometh because of their yielding their hearts unto God*" (Helaman 3:35, italics added). To "yield [our] hearts unto God" is to inquire diligently to know the mind and will of the Almighty; to give way to and follow the impressions of the Spirit; to have no will but God's will; to have an eye single to the glory of God. Thus a revelation given in December of 1832 stressed to the Saints that *"if your eye be single to my glory, your whole bodies shall be filled with light,* and there shall be no darkness in you; and that body which is filled with light comprehendeth all things. Therefore, *sanctify yourselves that your minds become single to God,* and the days will come that you shall see him; for he will unveil his face unto you, and it shall be in his own time, and in his own way, and according to his own will." (D&C 88:67–68, italics added.) Truly "sanctification . . . is just and true, to all those who love and serve God with all their mights, minds, and strength" (D&C 20:31).

Holiness

To ancient Israel the word of Jehovah was clear and direct: "I am the Lord your God: ye shall therefore sanctify yourselves, and ye shall be holy; for I am holy" (Leviticus 11:44). The Lord God desires that we become even as he is, and thus he has provided special assistance for us. As we have discussed, he has provided a member of the Godhead who is sent to prepare men and women for the greater revelation of the Father and the Son. In addition, the organization and teachings of the Church make opportunities for sanctifying service readily available. Members of the earthly kingdom are to "practise virtue and holiness" (D&C 38:24; 46:33), to "manifest before the church, and also before the elders, by a godly walk and conversation, that they are worthy of it, that there may be works and faith agreeable to the holy scriptures – walking in holiness before the Lord" (D&C 20:69). We meet together as a people for reproof, for correction, for instruction, and for inspiration. In fact, the Lord has directed that when we "are assembled together, [we] shall instruct and edify each other, that [we] may know how to act and direct [the] church, how to act upon the points of [his] law and commandments. . . . And thus," the Lord continued to the early Saints, "ye shall become instructed in the law of my church, and be sanctified by that which ye have received, and ye shall bind yourselves to act in all holiness before me." (D&C 43:8–9.)

To be holy is to be whole, entire, complete. The Holy Ghost thus works to make of us finished products, beings of light and truth who have fulfilled the measure of their creation. Sanctification is a condition. And sanctification is a process. In a day yet future the faithful will stand before God in complete confidence, totally and permanently absolved from the taints of mortality, absolutely free from sins and sinfulness. They will be sanctified. But that ultimate state of sanctification is not to be enjoyed in its fulness in this life. "Some suppose," President Brigham Young said, "that they can in the flesh be sanctified body and spirit and become so pure that they will never again feel the effects of the power of the adversary of truth. Were it possible for a person to attain to this degree of perfection in the flesh, he could not die neither remain in a world where sin predominates. Sin has entered into the world, and death by sin. I think we shall more or less feel the effects of sin so long as we live, and finally have to pass the ordeals of death." (*Journal of Discourses,* 10:173.) President Young later taught that "the power of God is greater than the power of the wicked one; and unless the Saints sin against light and knowledge, and wilfully neglect their plain and well-understood duties, . . . the Spirit is sure to prevail over the flesh, and ultimately succeeds in sanctifying the tabernacle for a residence in the presence of God." (*Journal of Discourses,* 11:237.) Such is a message of hope, a message of rejoicing.

Conclusion

The Holy Ghost is the sanctifier. One of his roles is to cleanse and purify the sons and daughters of God and thereby make them fit and able to go where Gods and angels are. To be sanctified is to partake of the spirit and attributes of holiness, to participate in the realm of the sacred. It is "by the blood" (Moses 6:60)—meaning the blood of Jesus the Savior—that we are sanctified. But it is through the cleansing medium of the Holy Ghost that the regenerating powers of that infinite atonement are extended to mortal man.

While Joseph Smith and Sidney Rigdon labored in their inspired translation of the Bible, and while pondering upon the doctrine of resurrection found in John 5, "the Lord touched the eyes of [their] understandings and they were opened, and the glory of the Lord shone round about." Then, the Prophet recorded, "we beheld the glory of the Son, on the right hand of the Father, and received of his fulness; and saw the holy angels, and them who are sanctified before his throne, worshiping God, and the Lamb, who worship him forever and ever." (D&C 76:19–21.) Such is the glorious destiny of the pure; such is the reward and opportunity available to those who have been sanctified by the Spirit.

11

Teaching and Learning by the Spirit

And the Spirit shall be given unto you by the prayer of faith; and if ye receive not the Spirit ye shall not teach.

—D&C 42:14

Because the things of God are to be seen and understood only by the power of the Spirit of God (1 Corinthians 2:11), it is vital that every gospel message be presented and received by that power if it is to find lodgement in the heart and produce the fruits of faith. Conversion and commitment follow on the heels of spiritual stirrings, and such stirrings come about only when the messenger is in tune with the Holy Spirit and when his message conveys that sacred influence. "Faith cometh by hearing," Paul explained, "and hearing by the word of God" (Romans 10:17). Joseph Smith expanded upon the words of Paul and observed that "faith comes by hearing the word of God, through the testimony of the servants of God; that testimony is always attended by the Spirit of prophecy and revelation" (*Teachings of the Prophet Joseph Smith*, p. 148).

"Ye Shall Not Teach"

Truly there is no greater calling in the Church and kingdom of God than that of teacher. Paul wrote: "God hath set some in the church, first apostles, secondarily prophets, thirdly teachers, after that miracles, then gifts of healings, helps, governments, diversities of tongues" (1 Corinthians 12:28). Note the priority of the list: teachers are mentioned just after those called to guide the destiny of the Church. Speaking in the context of Paul's comment and of the angel's statement to John that "the testimony of Jesus is the spirit of prophecy" (Revelation 19:10), Elder Bruce R. McConkie said: "After Apostles and prophets come teachers. Every teacher is expected to be a prophet and to know for himself of the truth and divinity of the work. Indeed, in the true sense, a teacher is greater than a prophet, for a teacher not only has the testimony of Jesus [for] himself [see Revelation 19:10], but he bears that testimony by teaching the gospel." (Bruce R. McConkie, "The Doctrinal Restoration," p. 2.)

Such a weighty assignment—that of gospel teacher—does not come without sober restrictions and sacred instructions. In a modern revelation the Savior explained that "the Spirit shall be given unto you by the prayer of faith; and if ye receive not the Spirit ye shall not teach" (D&C 42:14). "All are to preach the Gospel," the Prophet Joseph Smith said, "by the power and influence of the Holy Ghost; and no man can preach the Gospel without the Holy Ghost" (*Teachings of the Prophet Joseph Smith*, p. 112). This principle seems to embody both a command and a prophecy. The Saints are specifically instructed that their teachings are to be prepared and delivered by the power of the Holy Ghost, since their message is not to be theirs alone, but his who is their principal. The prophetic word is sure and the outcome is true and faithful: if the gospel teacher does not present his message by the power of the Holy Ghost, then "he will not teach." That is, he will not teach in the purest gospel sense—he will not teach in the manner the Lord has prescribed, will not communicate Spirit to spirit, will not edify, will not enlighten.

The Lord asks a question of the Saints, a question whose answer is vital to the matter of teaching the gospel. "Wherefore, I the Lord ask you this question—unto what were ye ordained?" He then declares:

To preach my gospel by the Spirit, even the Comforter which was sent forth to teach the truth. . . .

Verily I say unto you, he that is ordained of me and sent forth to preach the word of truth by the Comforter, in the Spirit of truth, doth he preach it by the Spirit of truth or some other way?

And if it be by some other way it is not of God.

And again, he that receiveth the word of truth, doth he receive it by the Spirit of truth or some other way?

If it be some other way it is not of God.

Therefore, why is it that ye cannot understand and know, that he that receiveth the word by the Spirit of truth receiveth it as it is preached by the Spirit of truth?

Wherefore, he that preacheth and he that receiveth, understand one another, and both are edified and rejoice together. (D&C 50:13-14, 17-22.)

It seems obvious that if a person teaches by the power of the Spirit, the experience—both the presentation and the reception of the message—is of God and will lead to mutual edification and enlightenment. But what other kind of learning experience might take place in the Church? What is "some other way" which is definitely designated by Deity as being "not of God"? In offering commentary upon these verses from section 50, particularly upon the manner in which someone might seek to convey the word of truth in "some other way," Elder Bruce R. McConkie observed:

If you teach the word of truth—now note, you are saying what is true, everything you say is accurate and right—by some other way than the Spirit, it is not of God. Now, what is the other way to teach than by the Spirit? Well, obviously, it is by the power of the intellect.

Suppose I came here tonight and delivered a great message on teaching, and I did it by the power of the intellect without any of the Spirit of God attending. Suppose that every word that I said was true, no error whatever, but it was an intellectual presentation. This revelation says: "If it be by some other way it is not of God" (D&C 50:18).

That is, God did not present the message through me because I used the power of the intellect instead of the power of the Spirit. Intellectual things—reason and logic—can do some good, and they can prepare the way, and they can get

the mind ready to receive the Spirit under certain circumstances. But conversion comes and the truth sinks into
the hearts of people only when it is taught by the power of
the Spirit. ("The Foolishness of Teaching," p. 9.)

As an illustration of the principle here involved, it is possible that
one of the Saints could stand in one of our meetings and read a seg-
ment from the standard works—neither adding to or taking therefrom—and yet his offering, though it be without blemish, not be of
God, because his heart was not right.

Mutual edification—spiritual education and divine refinement
—is a process, then, which is accomplished through an inspiring
teaching and inspired hearers. It is of God. "To enjoy the light and
power of the Holy Ghost," President Brigham Young taught, is
ever the prayer of the Saints, "but the preacher does not need it
any more than the hearers. The preacher needs the power of the
Holy Ghost to deal out to each heart a word in due season, and the
hearers need the Holy Ghost to bring forth the fruits of the
preached word of God to his glory." (*Journal of Discourses,*
8:167.)

Obtaining the Word

One cannot teach what he does not know. One cannot preach
the gospel with power if he does not know the gospel. And thus the
divine directive came to Hyrum Smith in the opening of the latter-
day work, a directive which states the prerequisites for spiritual
power: "Seek not to declare my word, but first seek to obtain my
word, and then shall your tongue be loosed; then, if you desire,
you shall have my Spirit and my word, yea, the power of God unto
the convincing of men. But now hold your peace; study my word
which hath gone forth among the children of men [the Bible], and
also study my word which shall come forth among the children of
men, or that which is now translating [the Book of Mormon]."
(D&C 11:21–22.)

This injunction is certainly in harmony with what we find in the
Book of Mormon. Of the sons of Mosiah, the Nephite record attests
that "they had waxed strong in the knowledge of the truth; for

they were men of a sound understanding and *they had searched the scriptures diligently, that they might know the word of God.* But this is not all; they had given themselves to much prayer, and fasting; therefore they had the spirit of prophecy, and the spirit of revelation, and *when they taught, they taught with power and authority of God.*" (Alma 17:2-3, italics added.) Testimony is born of knowledge. Thus "the sanctity of a true testimony should inspire a thoughtful care as to its use. That testimony is not . . . to be voiced merely to 'fill up the time' in a public meeting; far less to excuse or disguise the speaker's poverty of thought or ignorance of the truth he is called to expound. . . . Of those who speak in his name, the Lord requires humility, not ignorance." (Joseph F. Smith, *Gospel Doctrine,* pp. 205-6.)

To ensure that his teachings receive the divine stamp of approval, the gospel teacher must also see to it that his message is pure and true and untainted—that it is the gospel. "And again, the elders, priests and teachers of this church shall teach the principles of my gospel, which are in the Bible and the Book of Mormon, in the which is the fulness of the gospel. And they shall observe the covenants and church articles to do them, and these shall be their teachings, as they shall be directed by the Spirit." (D&C 42:12-13.) In our standard works—which now include the Doctrine and Covenants and the Pearl of Great Price—when supplemented with the words of modern prophets and Apostles, we have a standard which directs all we should teach in the Church. These books of holy writ constitute the canon of scripture, the rule of faith and doctrine against which truth and error are to be measured. Those who teach the message of the Restoration are to teach "none other things than that which the prophets and apostles have written, and that which is taught them by the Comforter through the prayer of faith" (D&C 52:9).

In this regard there is both a warning and a promise held out by our prophet-leaders. In 1938 President J. Reuben Clark, Jr., stressed to Church educators that "your chief interest, your essential and all but sole duty, is to teach the gospel of the Lord Jesus Christ as that has been revealed in these latter days. You are to teach this gospel, using as your sources and authorities the standard works of the Church and the words of those whom God has called to lead his people in these last days." He warned, "You are

not, whether high or low, to intrude into your work your own pe-
culiar philosophy, no matter what its source or how pleasing or ra-
tional it seems to you to be. To do so would be to have as many different churches as we have seminaries—and that is chaos." ("The
Charted Course of the Church in Education," p. 253.) In what is a
marvelous recommendation for gospel teachers to see to it that they
teach from the standard works, Elder Bruce R. McConkie wrote:

> Those who preach by the power of the Holy Ghost use
> the scriptures as their basic source of knowledge and doc-
> trine. They begin with what the Lord has before revealed to
> other inspired men. But it is the practice of the Lord to give
> added knowledge to those upon whose hearts the true mean-
> ings and intents of the scriptures have been impressed. Many
> great doctrinal revelations come to those who preach from the
> scriptures. When they are in tune with the Infinite, the Lord
> lets them know, first, the full and complete meaning of the
> scriptures they are expounding, and then he ofttimes ex-
> pands their views so that new truths flood in upon them, and
> they learn added things that those who do not follow such a
> course can never know. (*The Promised Messiah*, pp. 515–
> 16.)

A Portion of the Word

To every man is given a needful portion. It is the will of heaven
that all men and women receive according to their ability to de-
cipher and digest eternal verities. This principle is illustrative of
both divine wisdom and divine mercy. People ought not receive
more than they are ready and prepared to receive; the Lord would
never want to drown his children in the living waters! The inspired
gospel teacher does not teach all that he knows. He does not seek
to overwhelm his listeners nor to impress the congregation with the
wealth of material at his command. To do so is contrary to the order of heaven and counterproductive to the purposes of God.

As we have seen, the Holy Ghost is a personal tutor. He
"knoweth all things" (D&C 42:17); he knows the hearts and
minds of all men and women and the readiness of individuals and

congregations to be taught the things of God. No one rushes into the presence of the Lord; likewise no one should be ushered prematurely into the realm of divine experience. Alma explained it thus: "It is given unto many to know the mysteries of God; nevertheless they are laid under a strict command that they shall not impart only *according to the portion of the word which he doth grant unto the children of men,* according to the heed and diligence which they give unto him" (Alma 12:9; italics added). Those charged with proclaiming the gospel message are to be sensitive to the Spirit, discerning enough to recognize that "portion of the word" suited to those being taught.

Those laboring as missionaries for the Church, for example, are given a specific commission to teach that portion of the word necessary to introduce sincere investigators to the message of the Restoration. They are not commissioned to teach doctrines that could be more easily understood and appreciated after baptism and the reception of the Holy Ghost. Their specific assignment is to "declare glad tidings," the tidings that the Lord has spoken anew in our day through modern prophets, and to proclaim that the truthfulness of the message may be tested through the Book of Mormon. "And of tenets thou shalt not talk, but thou shalt declare repentance and faith on the Savior, and remission of sins by baptism, and by fire, yea, even the Holy Ghost." (D&C 19:29, 31.) We are to teach those outside the Church how to get into the Church. Thereafter, when they have been given the gift of the Holy Ghost, they may grow up into a fulness of understanding (see D&C 39:6).

The Lord explained to Joseph Smith and Sidney Rigdon that "the time has verily come that it is necessary and expedient in me that you should open your mouths in proclaiming my gospel, the things of the kingdom, expounding the mysteries thereof out of the scriptures, *according to that portion of Spirit and power which shall be given unto you,* even as I will" (D&C 71:1, italics added). This points toward the Lord's system of prerequisites—the principle that the things of God are to be presented and received in a certain order, that some things should and must be delivered in their proper sequence if edification is to occur and conversion by the power of the Holy Ghost is to take place. An account of a conversation between Peter and Clement is particularly insightful in this regard. Peter is reported to have instructed his younger companion that "the teaching of all doctrine has a certain order: there are some things which must be delivered first, others in the second place, and others in the third, and so on, everything in its order. If these things be delivered in their order they become plain; but if they be brought forward out of order, they will seem to be spoken against reason." (Cited in Hugh W. Nibley, *Since Cumorah*, p. 110; see also JST, Matthew 7:9–11.)

Thus, as the Prophet Joseph Smith warned, "it is not always wise to relate all the truth. Even Jesus, the Son of God, had to refrain from doing so, and had to restrain His feelings many times for the safety of Himself and His followers, and had to conceal the righteous purposes of His heart in relation to many things pertaining to His Father's kingdom." (*Teachings of the Prophet Joseph Smith*, p. 392.) "Remember," the Lord cautioned the Saints in our day, "that that which cometh from above is sacred, and must be spoken with care, and by constraint of the Spirit; and in this there is no condemnation" (D&C 63:64). The duty of the gospel teacher is to seek the Spirit of the Lord; to attend to the promptings and direction of that Spirit in regard to those to be taught; and to deliver the message under that same sacred influence. The Lord has instructed that after adequate and appropriate study and prayer, we are to "treasure up in [our] minds continually the words of life, and it shall be given unto [us] in the very hour that portion that shall be meted unto every man" (D&C 84:85).

Bearing Pure Testimony

The teacher's divine commission has been clearly articulated by the scriptures and by living prophets. He or she is to teach the gospel of Jesus Christ. It is to be taught out of the standard works and from the words of the living oracles. It is to be taught by the power of the Holy Ghost. It is to be applied to the life situations of the listeners, thus "likening the scriptures" unto the Saints. Finally, and as the capstone of the teaching enterprise, the teacher is to bear witness, by the power of the Holy Ghost, that what has been taught is true. Faith is developed and commitment is built as a result of testimony, pure and solid testimony. Alma the Younger left the judgment seat to confine himself wholly to the preaching of the gospel, "seeing no way that he might reclaim [the wandering Saints] save it were in bearing down in pure testimony against them" (Alma 4:19). The gospel teacher is to "declare the word with truth and soberness" (Alma 42:31). That is, he is to be true to the message delivered to him.

The Holy Ghost is the converter. The gospel teacher has much to do in the preparation of the lesson, the search of the scriptures, the declaration of the truth; but the Holy Ghost is the converter. And the gospel teacher must never forget this. He or she must never seek to usurp the role of the Spirit nor upstage him whose influence results in renewal and righteousness. The person who bears pure testimony never seeks for cheap substitutes for the Spirit. He never relies upon methodologies which might confuse sentimentality with spirituality, emotional display with edification. His witness is more than story, and his testimony is more than an expression of gratitude. He tries the virtue of the word of God (Alma 31:5), trusts in the power of the scriptures and the words of the prophets to penetrate to the heart of his listeners, and bears witness of his message with sincerity and with soberness.

We come to perfect our witness and develop and nurture the same in others when we are able to bear specific witness, when we are able to bear testimony not alone that the work in which we are engaged is true but also that the message we have presented and the doctrines we have expounded are true. Alma serves as a pattern for all who teach the gospel. Having spoken at length to the people of Zarahemla, having presented a type of spiritual checklist to the Saints; and having asked over forty questions of them by which they might assess their standing before their Maker, Alma added:

> For I am called to speak after this manner, according to the holy order of God, which is in Christ Jesus; yea, I am commanded to stand and testify unto this people the things which have been spoken by our fathers concerning the things which are to come.
>
> And this is not all. *Do ye not suppose that I know of these things myself? Behold, I testify unto you that I do*

know that these things whereof I have spoken are true. And how do ye suppose that I know of their surety?

Behold, I say unto you they are made known unto me by the Holy Spirit of God. Behold, I have fasted and prayed many days that I might know these things of myself. And now I do know of myself that they are true; for the Lord God hath made them manifest unto me by his Holy Spirit; and *this is the spirit of revelation which is in me.* (Alma 5:44-46, italics added.)

"The crowning, convincing, converting power of gospel teaching," wrote Elder Bruce R. McConkie, "is manifest when an inspired teacher says, 'I know by the power of the Holy Ghost, by the revelations of the Holy Spirit to my soul, that the doctrines I have taught are true.' This divine seal of approval makes the spoken word binding upon the hearers. . . . It should be added that when the Lord's servants preach in power, by the promptings of the Holy Spirit, the Lord adds his own witness to the truth of their words. That witness comes in the form of signs and gifts and miracles. Such are always found when the preached word, given in power, is believed by hearers with open hearts." (*The Promised Messiah,* pp. 516-17.)

President Brigham Young has left us the following regarding the impact of pure testimony on conversion:

I had only travelled a short time to testify to the people, before I learned this one fact, that you might prove doctrine from the Bible till doomsday, and it would merely convince a people, but would not convert them. You might read the Bible from Genesis to Revelation, and prove every iota that you advance, and that alone would have no converting influence upon the people. Nothing short of a testimony by the power of the Holy Ghost would bring light and knowledge to them—bring them in their hearts to repentance. Nothing short of that would ever do. You have frequently heard me say that I would rather hear an Elder, either here or in the world, speak only five words accompanied by the power of God, and they would do more good than to hear long sermons without the Spirit. That is true, and we know it. (*Journal of Discourses,* 5:327.)

Conclusion

Teaching is the Master's art. It is what Jesus did. It would not seem to be appropriate to speak of him as a gospel executive. Rather he was a teacher. And in his Church, teaching is what we do. We do it well when we do it in the way he did it; we do it in the way he did it when we are led and directed by the power of the Spirit. Those who teach by the power of the Holy Ghost echo and reflect the word and will of him who is eternal; they are agents of the Lord, who is their principal. They have no doctrine of their own to proclaim; their doctrine is his whom they represent. There can be no doubt that if those called and empowered to teach the gospel in the Lord's Church—though weak and simple in the eyes of the worldly wise (see D&C 1:19, 23)—always did so by the power of the Holy Ghost, edification and enlightenment and communion with the infinite would increasingly be the order of the day among the Latter-day Saints.

12

Approved of the Lord: The Holy Spirit of Promise

For these overcome, by their faith and their works,
Being tried in their life-time, as purified gold,
And seal'd by the spirit of promise, to life,
By men called of God, as was Aaron of old.
                                    —*Joseph Smith*

History is a fickle judge: a man deemed a hero in our day may be viewed in disgrace by our children, while he who was shunned, like Lazarus who begged at the rich man's gate, may find those who once scorned him begging his favor. A composer or artist may go unrecognized in his own lifetime, only to be acclaimed a master of timeless works in future years, while those enjoying the highest plaudits of their contemporaries may soon be forgotten or their works spurned. Seeking the approval of our fellowmen may be of all labors the most fruitless. Those willing to dance the devil's tune and to hear the cheers and applause of the multitudes have been warned that they shall yet be "despised by those that flattered them" (D&C 121:20). Like Korihor, when they stumble they will be trodden under the feet of those whose favor they so foolishly courted.

It is God's approval that good people seek, and his alone. There is no better measure of heaven's sanction of earthly deeds than the quiet peace which evidences the companionship of the Holy Ghost. The Holy Ghost is a spiritual aristocrat who will not company with the unholy or unclean. His ratifying seal of approval is readily placed upon all that is worthy of the divine presence and is quickly taken from that which is an offense or an affront to God. It is to this doctrine of the holy seal of promise, this doctrine by which we come to know that we are approved of God, that we now turn our attention.

God Will Not Be Deceived

It is a vice of good people to judge too kindly, to trust too quickly. The best of men have been betrayed. The Lord warned Joseph Smith that he would not always be able to "tell the wicked from the righteous" (D&C 10:37). With God it is not so; to him are known the hearts and thoughts of all men (D&C 6:16), and that which is known to God is known also to the Holy Ghost, for "the Comforter knoweth all things" (D&C 42:17). "Everlasting covenant was made," Joseph Smith explained, "between three personages before the organization of this earth, and relates to their dispensation of things to men on the earth; these personages, according to Abraham's record, are called God the first, the Creator; God the second, the Redeemer; and God the third, the witness or Testator" (*Teachings of the Prophet Joseph Smith,* p. 190). Not only does the Holy Ghost burn the testimony of truth into the hearts of men as if by fire, but he is also called upon to attest to the true condition of their souls. It is the Holy Ghost that ratifies or approves all that has weight and measure in heaven. Men may deceive each other, but there is no deceiving the Holy Ghost.

It is an absolute verity that no unclean thing can enter into the kingdom of God. "Therefore nothing entereth into his rest," the Savior declared, "save it be those who have washed their garments in my blood, because of their faith, and the repentance of all their sins, and their faithfulness unto the end" (3 Nephi 27:19). That same purity of soul is prerequisite to enjoying and exercising the power of the priesthood that is properly designated as "the Holy Priesthood, after the Order of the Son of God" (D&C 107:3), its very name affirming the necessity of holiness and order in all of its functions. Again, it is an absolute verity that the powers of heaven cannot be controlled nor handled save it be upon the principles of righteousness (D&C 121:36). In like manner, the Holy Spirit or

Holy Ghost is designed to stand as a constant reminder that his Spirit, its blessings and influence, cannot be enjoyed or retained independent of holiness.

Where there is no holiness there is no Holy Spirit. "The gift of the Holy Ghost by the laying on of hands cannot be received through the medium of any other principle than the principle of Righteousness," Joseph Smith explained (*Words of Joseph Smith,* p. 3). That which is holy is sacred rather than secular; it is that which has been "set apart," "consecrated," or "dedicated" to God. Those enjoying the companionship of the Holy Ghost are those who have experienced the union of two holy spirits. The Holy Ghost is not contentious and does not "strive" with man. Such is the labor of the Light or Spirit of Christ. When the struggle has ended, then the Holy Ghost—so beautifully symbolized in the appearance of the dove—enters, bringing a quiet peace in his wake. Such a Spirit cannot be deceived. When we open our doors to sin and discord, this Holy Spirit leaves as quietly and quickly as it came.

The Holy Spirit of Promise

Anything that we desire to lay claim to in the world to come must be "sealed" by the Holy Spirit of Promise. That is, the Holy Ghost must place his ratifying seal of approval upon it—a seal that attests that the conditions of the covenant, whatever the nature of it may have been, have been kept with exactness and honor. The standard is undeviating. "All covenants, contracts, bonds, obligations, oaths, vows, performances, connections, associations, or expectations, that are not made and entered into and sealed by the Holy Spirit of promise . . . are of no efficacy, virtue, or force in and after the resurrection from the dead" (D&C 132:7).

The ordinance of baptism provides an appropriate illustration of the principle. The scriptures liken baptism to the gate that opens to the celestial kingdom (D&C 76:51). As it takes the right key to open a door, so it takes the right baptism to admit one to the heavenly kingdom. For a baptism to be of "efficacy, virtue, or force" in the world to come it must conform to the revealed pattern. The divine pattern requires that baptism be by immersion in order that it symbolize the burial of Christ and his coming forth into a newness of life. A valid baptism must also be performed by the proper priesthood authority under the direction of one holding the keys—the directing or supervisory authority over this ordinance. If these conditions have been met and if the one being baptized has faith in Christ and His redeeming sacrifice and has properly repented of his sins, his baptism constitutes a gate through which he may enter the celestial kingdom. Such a baptism is approved of the Lord and bears the seal of the Holy Spirit of Promise to attest to its genuineness.

It is the Holy Ghost in his role as the Holy Spirit of Promise that attests to the legitimacy of every claim to a valid baptism. Because men can and do deceive one another, the responsibility to ratify the legitimacy of a baptism—or any other gospel ordinance, for that matter—must rest with God, and so it does. It rests with the Holy Ghost, the third member of the Godhead, to approve every claim to a valid baptism. There are no exceptions. It is for him alone to attest that the faith was authentic, the repentance real, and the conditions of the covenant met. In all instances in which this is the case, the Holy Ghost grants the promise that the ordinances will carry full weight and measure in the world to come—that is, he places his ratifying seal upon it. Thus his title, "Holy Spirit of Promise."

As with baptism, so with marriage. If a couple kneels in worthiness, clasping hands across an altar in the house of the Lord to be "sealed" for time and eternity, that ordinance is of immediate effect. Theirs is the promise of an eternal marriage. Yet should they in future years slip away from the sacred covenants made in the temple, their promise of eternal union may slip away also. Unworthiness or neglect will break the seal. Again, the principle is that no unclean thing can enter the kingdom of God. Repentance will of course repair that seal, and should a couple have married without having made the proper spiritual preparations, they too, through complete and proper repentance, can come to merit that seal. Yet all must understand that God will not be mocked—there will be no unworthiness in heaven.

The principle here involved is a manifestation of the law of justification. The law requires that there be no unearned blessings, that heaven have no favorites, that none be excused from complying with the gospel standard, that no sins be winked at. Should David plot against Uriah's life and steal his wife, David will lose his exaltation (D&C 132:39), notwithstanding the fact that every Bible reader has come to love him. None are granted license to sin; no wickedness is approved of the Lord. To be justified ultimately in the gospel sense is to be worthy to lay claim to heaven's blessings. Thus "all covenants, contracts, bonds, obligations, oaths, vows, performances, connections, associations, or expectations" must be sealed by the Holy Spirit of Promise (D&C 132:7). To "just about" live a commandment is to just about have claim upon the blessings that come from conforming to it. The Holy Ghost is justified in placing his ratifying or approving seal only upon those hopes and actions worthy of a place in heaven, and without that seal the person will have no place in heaven.

There is much concern on the part of some relative to the cancellation of sealings, with attendant feelings that someone has "gotten away" with something. Such may be the case in mortality for a time and a season, but such is never the case in the worlds to come. A humorous story from the days of Brigham Young illustrates: A disgruntled woman wrote demanding that her name be removed from the records of the Church. A clerk penned the following reply: "I have this day examined the records of baptisms for the remission of sins . . . and not being able to find (your) name recorded therein I was saved the necessity of erasing your name therefrom. You may therefore consider that your sins have not been remitted." (Ronald K. Esplin, "Historical Vignettes," *Church News*, 24 January 1976.)

None Are Exempt from Complying
with the Gospel Law

One of the greatest heresies ever imposed upon the gospel message is the idea that salvation comes by grace alone. Such a doctrine claims and praises Jesus as "Savior" while rejecting him as Lord, as Judge, and as the Just and Holy One. It promises salvation from hell without freedom from sin, faith without faithfulness, and it suggests that intellectual assent supplants wholehearted obedience. It is a doctrine whereby we pledge allegiance without paying our taxes. A sister heresy finds its way into the Church and kingdom of God, that being the idea that a couple who have been married in the temple then have license to sin within certain bounds with impunity.

A misinterpretation of D&C 132:26 has given encouragement to some who are obviously spiritually unstable to justify committing sin. The passage reads as follows:

> Verily, verily, I say unto you, if a man marry a wife according to my word, and they are sealed by the Holy Spirit of promise, according to mine appointment, and he or she shall commit any sin or transgression of the new and everlasting covenant whatever, and all manner of blasphemies, and if they commit no murder wherein they shed innocent blood, yet they shall come forth in the first resurrection, and enter into their exaltation; but they shall be destroyed in the flesh and shall be delivered unto the buffetings of Satan unto the day of redemption, saith the Lord God.

Contextually this passage has exclusive reference to those who have received the fulness of temple ordinances and have had "exaltation . . . sealed upon their heads." These are they to whom the Lord, through his anointed servant, has promised: "Ye shall come forth in the first resurrection . . . and shall inherit thrones, kingdoms, principalities, and powers, dominions, all heights and depths." (D&C 132:19.) The above promise is given to them, and to them alone. But even this does not suggest that they can sin with impunity. It simply affirms that those who have received the fulness of gospel ordinances and who have in fact had their calling and election made sure still have the capacity to sin and the right and privilege to repent. In their instance, however, it would appear that because of the sacred covenants they have made and because of the spiritual outpouring they have enjoyed, their repentance, which is possible if their transgressions are not too severe, may embrace suffering that goes far beyond that known to the generality of mankind. (See *Teachings of the Prophet Joseph Smith,* p. 128; Bruce R. McConkie, *Doctrinal New Testament Commentary,* 3:342–47; *A New Witness for the Articles of Faith,* p. 232.)

Now, this passage, which President Joseph Fielding Smith said is "the most abused passage in any scripture" (*Doctrines of Salvation*, 2:95), hardly suggests that anyone is getting away with anything. Holiness is ever the standard of heaven and the idea of sin is abhorrent to its citizenry. As to mortality, this is a probationary estate and all must exercise the utmost caution, for "there is a possibility that man may fall from grace and depart from the living God; therefore let the church take heed and pray always, lest they fall into temptation; yea, and even let those who are sanctified take heed also" (D&C 20:32–34).

The Second Comforter

In writing of Helaman, grandson of Alma, Mormon observed that "he had two sons. He gave unto the eldest the name of Nephi, and unto the youngest, the name of Lehi." And then Mormon added this fascinating note: "And *they began to grow up unto the Lord.*" (Helaman 3:21, italics added.) In the dedicatory prayer of the Kirtland Temple, Joseph Smith, in like manner, pleaded with the Lord that the Saints might *"grow up in thee, and receive a fulness of the Holy Ghost,* and be organized according to thy laws, and be prepared to obtain every needful thing" (D&C 109:14–15, italics added). The role of the Holy Ghost is to lead men and women to the point of illumination and inspiration at which they are ready to be ushered into the presence of the Father and the Son. Joseph Smith, in paraphrasing the Savior's words concerning the ministry of the Spirit, said: He "shall bring all things to remembrance, whatsoever things I have said unto you; *he shall teach you until ye come to me and my Father*" (*Words of Joseph Smith*, pp. 14–15, italics and modern punctuation added). The Prophet thus taught the brethren in the School of the Elders that "after any portion of the human family are made acquainted with the important fact that there is a God, who has created and does uphold all things, the extent of their knowledge respecting his character and glory will depend upon their diligence and faithfulness in seeking after him, until, like Enoch, the brother of Jared, and Moses, they shall obtain faith in God, and power with him to behold him face to face" (*Lectures on Faith,* 2:55).

Jesus taught of two comforters. The first, the Holy Ghost, he called "another Comforter," he himself being the other comforter. Speaking of himself, the Lord said, "I will not leave you comfortless: I will come to you." (John 14:15–18.) "He that hath my commandments," he explained, "and keepeth them, he it is that loveth me: and he that loveth me shall be loved of my Father, and I will love him, and will manifest myself to him" (John 14:21). Further, "if a man love me, he will keep my words: and my Father will love him, and we will come unto him, and make our abode with him" (John 14:23). "The appearing of the Father and the Son, in that verse [John 14:23]," the Prophet explained, "is a personal appearance; and the idea that the Father and the Son dwell in a man's heart is an old sectarian notion, and is false" (D&C 130:3). In offering further commentary upon these verses, the Prophet Joseph taught:

> When the Lord has thoroughly proved [a man], and finds that the man is determined to serve Him at all hazards, then the man will find his calling and his election made sure, then it will be his privilege to receive the other Comforter, which the Lord hath promised the Saints. . . .
>
> Now what is this other Comforter? It is no more nor less than the Lord Jesus Christ Himself; and this is the sum and substance of the whole matter; that when any man obtains this last Comforter, he will have the personage of Jesus Christ to attend him, or appear unto him from time to time, and even He will manifest the Father unto him, and they will take up their abode with him, and the visions of the heavens will be opened unto him, and the Lord will teach him face to face, and he may have a perfect knowledge of the mysteries of the Kingdom of God; and this is the state and place the ancient Saints arrived at when they had such glorious visions. (*Teachings of the Prophet Joseph Smith,* pp. 150–51.)

Similarly, Elder Bruce R. McConkie has written of this transcendent reality:

It is the privilege of all those who have made their calling and election sure to see God; to talk with him face to face; to commune with him on a personal basis from time to time. These are the ones upon whom the Lord sends the Second Comforter. Their inheritance of exaltation and eternal life is assured, and so it becomes with them here and now in this life as it will be with all exalted beings in the life to come. They become the friends of God and converse with him on a friendly basis as one man speaks to another. (*The Promised Messiah,* p. 584.)

Receiving the Second Comforter is an additional blessing, a further spiritual endowment available to those who make their calling and election sure. That is to say, one may indeed make his calling and election sure—may receive the certain promise from God that his salvation is assured—and yet not enjoy the blessings of the Second Comforter. There are "those whose callings and election have been made sure who have never exercised the [additional] faith nor exhibited the righteousness which would enable them to commune with the Lord on the promised basis." (Bruce R. McConkie, *The Promised Messiah,* p. 586.) On the other hand, if one qualifies for the presence of the Son, or as President Joseph Fielding Smith expressed it, "if a man gets knowledge enough to have the companionship of the Son of God, the chances are his call and election would be sure" (*Doctrines of Salvation,* 1:55).

For the present, these supernal gifts and blessings are reserved for but few of earth's inhabitants. In writing of a day yet future, Jeremiah declared with prophetic precision:

Behold, the days come, saith the Lord, that I will make a new covenant with the house of Israel, and with the house of Judah:

Not according to the covenant that I made with their fathers in the day that I took them by the hand to bring them out of the land of Egypt; which my covenant they brake, although I was an husband unto them, saith the Lord:

But this shall be the covenant that I will make with the house of Israel; After those days, saith the Lord, I will put my law in their inward parts, and write it in their hearts; and will be their God, and they shall be my people.

And they shall teach no more every man his neighbour, and every man his brother, saying, Know the Lord: for they shall all know me, from the least of them unto the greatest of them, saith the Lord: for I will forgive their iniquity, and I will remember their sin no more. (Jeremiah 31:31–34.)

Of this text, Joseph Smith said: "The day must come when no man need say to his neighbor, Know ye the Lord; for all shall know Him (who remain) from the least to the greatest." Then he asked: "How is this to be done? It is to be done by this sealing power, and the other Comforter spoken of, which will be manifest by revelation." (*Teachings of the Prophet Joseph Smith,* p. 149.)

In our own day we have been instructed to "seek the face of the Lord always" (D&C 101:38), with the promise that "inasmuch as you strip yourselves from jealousies and fears, and humble yourselves before me, for ye are not sufficiently humble, the veil shall be rent and you shall see me and know that I am" (D&C 67:10). Indeed, the promised reward is certain to those who seek him in patient maturity and quiet dignity: "Verily, thus saith the Lord: It shall come to pass that every soul who forsaketh his sins and cometh unto me, and calleth on my name, and obeyeth my voice, and keepeth my commandments, shall see my face and know that I am" (D&C 93:1; compare 88:67–68).

Scriptural Examples of Those Approved of the Lord

To Alma the word of Jehovah came peacefully but forcefully: "Thou art my servant; and I covenant with thee that thou shalt have eternal life" (Mosiah 26:20). Alma thereby made his calling and election sure; he received the more sure word of prophecy; his life was approved of God and he was sealed by the Holy Spirit of Promise to exaltation.

In the meridian of time Peter, James, and John enjoyed like privileges. In speaking of their experience on the Mount of Transfiguration and thus of the basis for their steadfastness in faith,

Peter observed: "We have not followed cunningly devised fables, when we made known unto you [the Saints to whom Peter is writing] the power and coming of our Lord Jesus Christ, but were eyewitnesses of his majesty. For he received from God the Father honour and glory, when there came such a voice to him from the excellent glory, This is my beloved Son, in whom I am well pleased. And this voice which came from heaven we heard, when we were with him in the holy mount [see Matthew 17:1-5]. *We have also a more sure word of prophecy;* whereunto ye do well that ye take heed, as unto a light that shineth in a dark place, until the day dawn, and the day star arise in your hearts." (2 Peter 1:16-19, italics added.)

"Now, wherein could they have a more sure word of prophecy," Joseph Smith asked, "than to hear the voice of God saying, 'This is my beloved Son'?"

> Now for the secret and grand key. Though they might hear the voice of God and know that Jesus was the Son of God, this would be no evidence that their election and calling was made sure, that they had part with Christ, and were joint heirs with Him. They then would want that more sure word of prophecy, that they were sealed in the heavens and had the promise of eternal life in the kingdom of God. Then, having this promise sealed unto them, it was an anchor to the soul, sure and steadfast. Though the thunders might roll and lightnings flash, and earthquakes bellow, and war gather thick around, yet this hope and knowledge would support the soul in every hour of trial, trouble and tribulation. Then knowledge through our Lord and Savior Jesus Christ is the grand key that unlocks the glories and mysteries of the kingdom of heaven. (*Teachings of the Prophet Joseph Smith,* p. 298.)

Moroni delivered one of the most poignant pleas to come unto Christ in all of scripture. In the process of doing so, he bore a powerful and persuasive testimony of his Lord and spoke of his relationship with that Lord.

> And now I, Moroni, bid farewell unto the Gentiles, yea, and also unto my brethren whom I love, until we shall meet

before the judgment-seat of Christ, where all men shall know that my garments are not spotted with your blood.

And then shall ye know that I have seen Jesus, and that he hath talked with me face to face, and that he told me in plain humility, even as a man telleth another in mine own language, concerning these things [concerning the power of faith and charity];

And now, I would commend you to seek this Jesus of whom the prophets and apostles have written, that the grace of God the Father, and also the Lord Jesus Christ, and the Holy Ghost, which beareth record of them, may be and abide in you forever. Amen. (Ether 12:38–39, 41.)

Elder Heber C. Kimball, one of the most devoted disciples of this dispensation, wrote of an experience in his life as follows:

My family having been gone about two months, during which time I heard nothing from them; our brethren being in prison; death and destruction following us everywhere we went; I felt very sorrowful and lonely. The following words came to my mind, and the Spirit said unto me, "write," which I did by taking a piece of paper and writing on my knee as follows. . . . Verily I say unto my servant Heber, thou art my son, in whom I am well pleased; for thou art careful to hearken to my words, and not transgress my law, nor rebel against my servant Joseph Smith, for thou hast a respect to the words of mine anointed, even from the least to the greatest of them; therefore thy name is written in heaven, no more to be blotted out for ever." (Orson F. Whitney, *Life of Heber C. Kimball,* p. 241.)

To his trusted secretary, William Clayton, Joseph the Prophet said: "Your life is hid with Christ in God, and so are many others. Nothing but the unpardonable sin can prevent you from inheriting eternal life for you are sealed up by the power of the Priesthood unto eternal life, having taken the step necessary for that purpose." (*History of the Church,* 5:391.) And it is to Joseph Smith himself that we turn for the pattern as to how it is that a man is sealed unto eternal life, and from whom we learn of the vital nature of obedience and sacrifice. "I am the Lord thy God," the Master said to the seer, "and will be with thee even unto the end of the world, and through all eternity; for verily I seal upon you your exaltation, and prepare a throne for you in the kingdom of my Father, with Abraham your father. Behold, I have seen your sacrifices, and will forgive all your sins; I have seen your sacrifices in obedience to that which I have told you." (D&C 132:49–50.)

The scriptural pronouncement to the Saints is consistent: Those who accept the covenant gospel, receive the ordinances of salvation, and endure in righteousness to the end of their days shall have eternal life. "If you keep my commandments and endure to the end," the Lord assured David Whitmer, "you shall have eternal life, which gift is the greatest of all the gifts of God" (D&C 14:7). "Blessed are they who are faithful and endure, *whether in life or in death,* for they shall inherit eternal life" (D&C 50:5, italics added). We strive daily to keep the commandments, to live worthy of the directing and sanctifying influences of the Holy Spirit. We long and labor for that peace which certifies that the Lord is pleased with us, that he has accepted of our offerings. We pursue the path of discipleship in a sane and balanced manner, never seeking to run before our file leaders or to be excessive in our zeal for the things of the Spirit. Our righteous obsession is to qualify for the highest of eternal possibilities. Indeed, we yearn for the certain assurance that the fulness of salvation will be ours. But if we do not formally receive the more sure word of prophecy before we face death and entrance into the next sphere, we rest secure in the promises of him who desires that we be his everlastingly. Thus,

> If we die in the faith, that is the same thing as saying that our calling and election has been made sure and that we will go on to eternal reward hereafter. As far as faithful members of the Church are concerned, they have charted a course leading to eternal life. This life is the time that is appointed as a probationary estate for men to prepare to meet God, and as far as faithful people are concerned, if they are in the line of their duty, if they are doing what they ought to do, although they may not have been perfect in this sphere, their

probation is ended. Now there will be some probation for
some other people hereafter. But for the faithful Saints of
God, now is the time and the day, and their probation is
ended with their death, and they will not thereafter depart
from the path. It is true, as the Prophet Joseph Smith said,
that there are many things that have to be done "even beyond the grave" to work out our salvation, but we'll stay in
the course and we will not alter from it if we have been true
and faithful in this life. (Bruce R. McConkie, remarks at the
funeral of S. Dilworth Young, 13 July 1981.)

Conclusion

The perfections of heaven's truths attest to their divine origin.
Such is surely the case with the eternal decree that all oaths, covenants, and promises must be sealed by the Holy Spirit of Promise.
Thus the unclean, the unholy, the impure will never find place in
the celestial worlds. Given that men are to be judged by their
works and their desires (D&C 137:9), we have a perfect confidence
that those doing the right thing for the right reason will be amply
rewarded, while those who did not do so because of circumstances
beyond their control will be rewarded in like measure. As to those
who feigned the form of godliness while denying the purpose and
power thereof, we can but observe that the glory of heaven is the
brighter by their absence. Men may deceive men, but no one can
nor ever will deceive God.

In this chapter baptism and marriage have been chosen as the
primary examples of the principles here involved. This but follows
the pattern of the scriptures. In Joseph Smith's prophetic description of the degrees of glory, he declares baptism as the gate to the
celestial kingdom. Having announced that it must be in the like-
ness of Christ's burial, he then declares that it is "by keeping the
commandments" that we are cleansed from sin. Thus we see that
it is the works of righteousness that breathe the breath of life into
the saving ordinances. To those who keep the commandments
comes the promise that they will be granted the gift of the Holy

Ghost "by the laying on of the hands of him who is ordained and sealed unto this power"; those who are exalted are the ones who "overcome" the world by faith, and "are sealed by the Holy Spirit of promise, which the Father sheds forth upon all those who are just and true." (D&C 76:51–53.)

The great revelation on eternal marriage follows the same pattern. It first teaches that the composite of all gospel covenants constitutes the new and everlasting covenant or the path of salvation. It then takes marriage as its example of "a" new and "an" everlasting covenant to teach the principle. Again we are taught that the proper ordinances must be performed, that they must be performed by or under the direction of one holding the keys, and that the candidates for celestial marriage must be and must continue to be worthy of the Holy Spirit. When such is the case, their marriage, as with all eternal covenants, is sealed by the Holy Spirit of Promise according to the holy order of heaven. (D&C 132:5–8.) Such is the system of salvation.

13

Grieving the Spirit

Know ye not that ye are the temple of God, and that the Spirit of God dwelleth in you? If any man defile the temple of God, him shall God destroy; for the temple of God is holy, which temple ye are.
— *1 Corinthians 3:16–17*

As there is order in the physical creation of all things, so there is order in their spiritual birth and development. As the morning sun rises gradually to its refulgent glory, so the light of the gospel must first chase away the night of unbelief, that it might gain ascendency over the souls of men. It is for the Light of Christ to attract the attention of those walking in the darkness. It is for the Light of Christ to bring those huddled in the shadows of sin to stand in its warming rays. It is not for the Holy Ghost to "strive" with those laden with sin any more than it is for the curious and spiritually untutored to be invited into holy places and be shown the sacred "hidden treasures" of eternity.

The baptism of water must precede the baptism of fire. As the ritual of washing must precede the ritual of anointing, so the process of cleansing must precede the outpouring of the Spirit. It is for the Light of Christ to invite and entice men to do good, while it is for the Holy Ghost to endow with power from on high those who have done good. It is the Light of Christ that prepares men and women to receive the Holy Ghost. Transgression will cause the Holy Spirit to withdraw, leaving the Light of Christ to vie for the attention of the wayward soul. Yet even continual and consistent

wickedness can cause the Spirit of Light to withdraw. "He that re-
pents not, from him shall be taken even the light which he has received; for my Spirit shall not always strive with man, saith the
Lord of Hosts" (D&C 1:33).

Holiness Before the Lord

"I am the Lord your God: ye shall therefore sanctify yourselves, and ye shall be holy; for I am holy" (Leviticus 11:44). Such
was the great command from Sinai, a command that ever has and
ever will stand at the heart of the covenant of salvation. Our God is
holy and our covenant is to be like him. His priesthood was known
to the ancients as "the Holy Priesthood, after the Order of the Son
of God" (D&C 107:3). The Book of Mormon peoples simply called
it the "holy order" (2 Nephi 6:2; Alma 6:8; 13:1, 8, 10, 11), while
modern revelation refers to it as the "holiest order of God" (D&C
84:18).

Many are called to hold this sacred authority, but few are chosen. "And why are they not chosen? Because their hearts are set so
much upon the things of this world, and aspire to the honors of
men, that they do not learn this one lesson—that the rights of the
priesthood are inseparably connected with the powers of heaven,
and that the powers of heaven cannot be controlled nor handled
only upon the principles of righteousness." The priesthood may be
conferred upon us; we may have claim upon an office therein; indeed, we may function in the authority of the priesthood; but to actually possess the power of God is quite another matter. "When
we undertake to cover our sins, or to gratify our pride, our vain
ambition, or to exercise control or dominion or compulsion upon
the souls of the children of men, in any degree of unrighteousness,
behold, the heavens withdraw themselves; the Spirit of the Lord is
grieved; and when it is withdrawn, Amen to the priesthood or the
authority of that man." (D&C 121:34–37.) Simply stated, where
there is no holiness there is no priesthood, no Holy Spirit of Promise or assurance of divine approval, no promptings from the Holy
Spirit, no right to draw upon any of the power associated with his
holy name.

Holy is constantly used as both an adjective and a noun in describing virtually every aspect of the kingdom of God. Our God is Man of Holiness (Moses 6:57), the other members of the Godhead being Christ or the Holy One and the Holy Ghost or Holy Spirit. The presence of God is to be sought in his holy house, his agents are holy angels, holy Apostles, holy prophets, holy oracles, and holy men. Such individuals function by the power and authority of his holy priesthood. We worship on his holy day, we espouse his most holy faith, we are gathered to holy lands where we are enjoined to stand in holy places. By command every member of the Church is to "esteem his brother as himself, and practise virtue and holiness" before God (D&C 38:24). Indeed, that which is not holy is not of God, and until it becomes so it cannot have the highest rewards of the eternal plan.

All that is unholy—all that is carnal, sensual, and devilish—is shut out from the presence of God. Thus all within the earthly kingdom are charged with the responsibility to teach their children the doctrine of repentance, for without repentance "they can in nowise inherit the kingdom of God, for no unclean thing can dwell there." (Moses 6:49, 57.) "I, the Lord, am angry with the wicked; I am holding my Spirit from the inhabitants of the earth" (D&C 63:32).

Giving Offense to the Spirit

All that is unholy or unclean is offensive to the Spirit. The scriptural metaphor for the body is a temple, which if polluted is subject not only to the loss of the Spirit but even to destruction. The Holy Ghost freely associates with those Saints who are worthy to enter the temple, while the Light of Christ assumes the responsibility to labor to bring people to such a state of holiness. The Psalmist conveyed this idea when he asked: "Who shall ascend into the hill of the Lord? or who shall stand in his holy place?" By way of response he said: "He that hath clean hands, and a pure heart; who hath not lifted up his soul unto vanity, nor sworn deceitfully. He shall receive the blessing from the Lord, and righteousness from the God of his salvation." (Psalm 24:3–5.)

The Holy Ghost is more easily offended than the Light of Christ, the companionship of the former being reserved for those who have purified the tabernacle of their soul to receive it. Nevertheless that light which comes from Christ—that light with which all men are born and which has been designated to strive with those in darkness, to bring them into the light—can also be sufficiently offended that it may weary and withdraw. The withdrawal of either Spirit is a most painful and difficult experience for those who have become accustomed to its light, warmth, and intelligence. Such, for instance, was the experience of Joseph Smith, Martin Harris, and others associated with the loss of the 116 pages of the Book of Mormon manuscript. In a subsequent revelation the Lord commanded Martin Harris to repent, "lest I humble you with my almighty power; and that you confess your sins, lest you suffer these punishments of which I have spoken [the reference being to the manner in which Christ suffered in Gethsemane and on Calvary], of which in the smallest, yea, even in the least degree you have tasted at the time I withdrew my Spirit" (D&C 19:20). Describing their feelings when the Spirit was withdrawn, the Prophet's mother, Lucy Mack Smith, said: "I well remember that day of darkness, both within and without. To us, at least, the heavens seemed clothed with blackness, and the earth shrouded with gloom. I have often said within myself, that if a continual punishment, as severe as that which we experienced on that occasion, were to be inflicted upon the most wicked characters who ever stood upon the footstool of the Almighty—if even their punishment were no greater than that, I should feel to pity their condition." (Lucy Mack Smith, *History of Joseph Smith*, p. 132.)

Indeed, the fruits of disobedience can be most bitter. Perhaps, however, the most common way in which the Spirit is offended is when the sacred tabernacle of a person's body is polluted by his transgressing the law of chastity. The Lord has warned that even the act of looking upon a woman to lust after her is sufficient to cause the Spirit to retreat, leaving such a state of darkness to engulf the offender that he will lose what light and testimony he had and find himself denying the faith (see D&C 42:23). Again in a subsequent revelation the Lord said, "Verily I say unto you, as I have said before, he that looketh on a woman to lust after her, or if any shall commit adultery in their hearts, they shall not have the Spirit, but shall deny the faith and shall fear'' (D&C 63:16).

Quench Not the Spirit

Because the intent is that the Spirit of God burn within every willing person as a holy fire, because it is our source of light and warmth, indeed, because the Lord's Spirit gives life to our spirits, Paul warned the Saints of the meridian day to "quench not the Spirit" (1 Thessalonians 5:19). Rather they were to "stir up ["stir to flame" in the New English Bible rendering] the gift of God" that had been given them (2 Timothy 1:6). "Let the peace of God rule in your hearts," he said. "Let the word of Christ dwell in you richly in all wisdom; teaching and admonishing one another in psalms and hymns and spiritual songs, singing with grace in your hearts to the Lord." (Colossians 3:15–16.) Having spoken by the spirit of prophecy, Jacob sounded the same warning among the Book of Mormon peoples. "Behold, will ye reject these words?" he asked. "Will ye reject the words of the prophets; and will ye reject all the words which have been spoken concerning Christ, after so many have spoken concerning him; and deny the good word of Christ, and the power of God, and the gift of the Holy Ghost, and quench the Holy Spirit, and make a mock of the great plan of redemption, which hath been laid for you? Know ye not that if ye will do these things, that the power of the redemption and the resurrection, which is in Christ, will bring you to stand with shame and awful guilt before the bar of God?" (Jacob 6:8–9.) In our own dispensation we have been instructed by the voice of the Lord to "build upon my rock, which is my gospel; deny not the spirit of revelation, nor the spirit of prophecy, for wo unto him that denieth these things" (D&C 11:24–25).

If we to whom the gift of the Holy Ghost has been given ignore the proddings of that Spirit and become callous to its promptings and impervious to its pleadings, we will be as those of whom the Savior said, "They draw near to me with their lips, but their hearts are far from me, they teach for doctrines the commandments of men, having a form of godliness, but they deny the power thereof"

(Joseph Smith – History 1:19). We must be true to and trusting of that which the Lord has given us. As to the declaring of that message to others, it ought be observed that "there is a spirit associated with the message we have been called to proclaim that cannot be experienced when we have departed from the message. The word of the Lord, we are told, is 'true and faithful' (D&C 66:11; Revelation 21:5), meaning that it is trustworthy and dependable. The true messenger must be equally loyal and trustworthy. To take license with the message is to offend that Spirit by which the message was revealed, and to lose the power by which it must be proclaimed. The core of true religion must ever be the submissiveness of the messenger to the message. He must speak as moved upon by the Holy Ghost. It is not a matter of what people want to hear, for the message is not of men but of God." (Joseph Fielding McConkie, *Prophets and Prophecy,* pp. 162-63.)

"When a man revolts against the work of God and against the counsels of his servants, and will not be subject to the Holy Ghost which dwells in him, he commits treason against God, and against his authority on the earth," stated Elder Heber C. Kimball, "and neither the Father, nor the Son, nor the Holy Ghost will take up their abode with such a man, and he may bid farewell to the guidance of good angels" (*Journal of Discourses,* 11:145).

The Sin Against the Holy Ghost

The Lord explained that many trials in life are to be overcome through patience, that the servants of God "may receive a more exceeding and eternal weight of glory, otherwise, *a greater condemnation*" (D&C 63:66, italics added). Indeed, the Saints of the Most High have been given the power to rise to celestial heights, to go where Gods and angels are. They also have the capacity – because of who they are, what they know, and what they have felt – to fall farther, to descend to spiritual depths beyond those who have never known the things of the Spirit, "for of him unto whom much is given much is required; and he who sins against the greater light shall receive the greater condemnation" (D&C 82:3). Mormon drew a lesson from the experiences of the descendants of Lehi which is timeless and timely. "And thus we can plainly discern," he taught, "that after a people have been once enlightened by the Spirit of God, and have had great knowledge of things pertaining to righteousness, and then have fallen away into sin and transgression, they become more hardened, and thus their state becomes worse than though they had never known these things" (Alma 24:30; compare 2 Peter 2:20–21).

In teaching the Pharisees, the Master warned that "all manner of sin and blasphemy shall be forgiven unto men who receive me and repent; but the blasphemy against the Holy Ghost, it shall not be forgiven unto men. And whosoever speaketh a word against the Son of Man, it shall be forgiven him; but whosoever speaketh against the Holy Ghost, it shall not be forgiven him; neither in this world; neither in the world to come." (JST, Matthew 12:26–27.) One would naturally think that the personal presence of the Lord or the ministry of angelic beings would have a more profound and lasting effect upon the soul than the witness of the Spirit. And yet it was Jesus himself who instructed his own: "I tell you the truth; it is expedient for you that I go away: for if I go not away, the Comforter will not come unto you" (John 16:7). A modern prophet explained:

> The Spirit of God speaking to the spirit of man has power to impart truth with greater effect and understanding than the truth can be imparted by personal contact even with heavenly beings. Through the Holy Ghost the truth is woven into the very fibre and sinews of the body so that it cannot be forgotten. So positive and powerful are the teachings of the Spirit that when a man receives this knowledge and partakes of this power of God, which can only come after receiving the covenants and obligations belonging to the new and everlasting covenant, and he then turns away from this knowledge and those covenants, he sins knowingly. (Joseph Fielding Smith, *Doctrines of Salvation,* 1:47–48.)

Satan is called Perdition, meaning he is the author of ruination and the father of lies. Those who bask in the light of heaven and come to know God, and who then sin against that light and come to fight the faith of their fathers with a viciousness and a vengeance known only to the ungodly—these become the *sons of perdition.* Their sin is blasphemy, contempt for and defiance against the Holy Ghost and his witness. (See Robert L. Millet and Joseph Fielding McConkie, *In His Holy Name,* pp. 70, 84.)

One of the most vivid descriptions of the sons of perdition in all of holy writ—the nature of their sin and their destiny—is contained in the Vision of the Glories. Joseph Smith and Sidney Rigdon recorded their glimpse of the ungodly as follows:

> And we saw a vision of the sufferings of those with whom [Satan] made war and overcame, for thus came the voice of the Lord unto us:
>
> Thus saith the Lord concerning all those who know my power, and have been made partakers thereof, and suffered themselves through the power of the devil to be overcome, and to deny the truth and defy my power—
>
> They are they who are the sons of perdition, of whom I say that it had been better for them never to have been born;
>
> For they are vessels of wrath, doomed to suffer the wrath of God, with the devil and his angels in eternity;
>
> Concerning whom I have said there is no forgiveness in this world nor in the world to come—
>
> Having denied the Holy Spirit after having received it, and having denied the Only Begotten Son of the Father, having crucified him unto themselves and put him to an open shame.
>
> These are they who shall go away into the lake of fire and brimstone, with the devil and his angels—
>
> And the only ones on whom the second death shall have any power;
>
> Yea, verily the only ones who shall not be redeemed [to a kingdom of glory] in the due time of the Lord, after the sufferings of his wrath. (D&C 76:30–38.)

"What must a man do to commit the unpardonable sin?" the Prophet Joseph Smith asked. "He must receive the Holy Ghost, have the heavens opened unto him, and know God, and then sin against Him. After a man has sinned against the Holy Ghost, there is no repentance for him. He has got to say that the sun does not shine while he sees it; he has got to deny Jesus Christ when the heavens have been opened unto him, and to deny the plan of salvation with his eyes open to the truth of it." But the sin is more than denial; it is more than inactivity in the church; it is more than losing one's testimony. As the revelations attest, such a person comes to *defy* the truth, to wage war against the Lord, His servants, and His work. The Prophet taught that such a one becomes an enemy to the Church of the Lamb, one who "hunts me, [who] seeks to kill me, and never ceases to thirst for my blood. He gets the spirit of the devil." (*Teachings of the Prophet Joseph Smith,* p. 358.)

It is of this spirit—a vile and vicious disposition wherein one would crucify the Son of Man again if he could—that the Lord speaks in modern revelation: "The blasphemy against the Holy Ghost, which shall not be forgiven in the world nor out of the world, is in that ye commit murder wherein ye shed innocent blood [the innocent blood of Christ] and assent unto my death, after ye have received my new and everlasting covenant" (D&C 132:27). The Apostle Paul likewise wrote to the Saints of his day regarding this heinous crime: "It is impossible," he stated, "for those who were once enlightened, and have tasted of the heavenly gift, and were made partakers of the Holy Ghost, and have tasted the good word of God, and the powers of the world to come, if they shall fall away, to renew them again unto repentance; seeing they crucify to themselves the Son of God afresh, and put him to an open shame" (Hebrews 6:4-6). Later in the same epistle Paul wrote of the sons of perdition as individuals who have "trodden under foot the Son of God, and hath counted the blood of the covenant, wherewith he was sanctified, an unholy thing, and hath done despite unto the spirit of grace" (Hebrews 10:29). Their pattern and their plight are ironic: they condemn and they destroy that which could save and settle them. "When once that light which was in them is taken from them, they become as much darkened as they were previously enlightened, and then, no marvel, if all their power should be enlisted against the truth, and they, Judas like, seek the destruction of those who were their greatest benefactors" (*Teachings of the Prophet Joseph Smith,* p. 67).

In counseling his errant son, Corianton, Alma emphasized the seriousness of sexual sin and then spoke of the sin of murder and the sin against the Holy Ghost. "For behold," he warned, "if ye deny the Holy Ghost when it once has had place in you, and ye know that ye deny it, behold, *this is a sin which is unpardonable*; yea, and whosoever murdereth against the light and knowledge of God, it is not easy for him to obtain forgiveness; yea, I say unto you, my son, that it is not easy for him to obtain a forgiveness" (Alma 39:5–6, italics added). Murder is a sin which is said to be *unforgivable*; it is a heinous crime against humanity, an offense not covered by the atoning blood of Christ and for which deliverance from hell in the world of spirits is possible only after much personal suffering (see D&C 42:18, 79; *Teachings of the Prophet Joseph Smith*, p. 339). "There are sins unto death," wrote Elder Bruce R. McConkie, "meaning spiritual death. There are sins for which there is no forgiveness, neither in this world nor in the world to come. There are sins which utterly and completely preclude the sinner from gaining eternal life. Hence there are sins for which repentance does not operate, sins that the atoning blood of Christ will not wash away, sins for which the sinner must suffer and pay the full penalty personally." (*A New Witness for the Articles of Faith*, p. 231.) The sin against the Holy Ghost is said to be *unpardonable* in that it is not covered by the atoning blood of Christ and because no amount of personal suffering can atone for or pardon the pernicious deed and make up for the misery and suffering to the Saints which inevitably follow in its wake.

The ultimate state of the sons of perdition has not been revealed. Indeed, regarding the nature and extent of their suffering, the revelations affirm that "the end, the width, the height, the depth, and the misery thereof, [we] understand not, neither any man except those who are ordained unto this condemnation" (D&C 76:44–48). What Joseph Smith did teach was that "the Lord never authorized [any] to say that the devil, his angels, or the sons of perdition, should ever be restored; for their state of destiny was not revealed . . . nor ever shall be revealed, save to those who are made partakers thereof: consequently those who teach this doctrine [that the sons of perdition will eventually be relieved from the punishment] have not received it of the Spirit of the Lord.

Truly Brother Oliver declared it to be the doctrine of devils. We, therefore, command that this doctrine be taught no more in Zion." (*Teachings of the Prophet Joseph Smith,* p. 24.)

The prophets have repeatedly taught that the cost of deliverance from the devil and death and hell is vigilance. Since one's state of mind and level of enjoyment hereafter is directly related to his directions and desires here, it follows that "no man can commit the unpardonable sin after the dissolution of the body" (*Teachings of the Prophet Joseph Smith,* p. 357). And so the command is ever before us: Watch and be ready! Take heed to yourselves! Endure in faithfulness to the end! In our day the Lord's directive to receive the words of his anointed as if from His own mouth is particularly relevant in assuring that the gates of hell do not prevail against us (D&C 1:38; 21:4-6). The Prophet Joseph warned and pleaded:

> O ye Twelve! and all Saints! profit by this important key —that in all your trials, troubles, temptations, afflictions, bonds, imprisonments and death, see to it, that you do not betray heaven; that you do not betray Jesus Christ; that you do not betray the brethren; that you do not betray the revelations of God. . . . Yea, in all your kicking and flounderings, see to it that you do not this thing, lest innocent blood be found upon your skirts, and you go down to hell. All other sins are not to be compared to sinning against the Holy Ghost, and proving a traitor to the brethren. (*Teachings of the Prophet Joseph Smith,* p. 156.)

Conclusion

It is a consummate privilege to receive the gift of the Holy Ghost. It is also a sacred obligation, one which must not be taken lightly. Those who have received this transcendent gift must labor with diligence to keep it, to refrain from those thoughts or practices which are inappropriate and unbecoming of a Saint, those things which are repulsive to God and offensive to his Holy Spirit. Holiness is a delicate and a fragile state, one which is approached and

achieved and maintained through obedience and commitment to
the principles and ordinances of the gospel, one which presup-
poses and requires the sanctifying and edifying influences of the
Holy Ghost. It requires decision and determination—staying on the
Lord's side of the line and enjoying the spiritual benefits which ac-
crue to those who follow him. President George Albert Smith explained:

> There are two influences in the world today, and have
> been from the beginning. One is an influence that is con-
> structive, that radiates happiness and builds character. The
> other influence is one that destroys, turns men into demons,
> tears down and discourages. We are all susceptible to both.
> The one comes from our Heavenly Father, and the other
> comes from the source of evil that has been in the world
> from the beginning, seeking to bring about the destruction of
> the human family. . . .
>
> My grandfather used to say to his family, "There is a line
> of demarkation, well defined, between the Lord's territory
> and the devil's. If you will stay on the Lord's side of the line
> you will be under his influence and will have no desire to do
> wrong; but if you cross to the devil's side of the line one
> inch, you are in the tempter's power, and if he is successful,
> you will not be able to think or even reason properly, be-
> cause you will have lost the Spirit of the Lord."
>
> When I have been tempted sometimes to do a certain
> thing, I have asked myself, "Which side of the line am I
> on?" If I determined to be on the safe side, the Lord's side, I
> would do the right thing every time. So when temptation
> comes, think prayerfully about your problem, and the influ-
> ence of the Spirit of the Lord will enable you to decide
> wisely. There is safety for us only on the Lord's side of the
> line.
>
> If you want to be happy, remember, that all happiness
> worthy of the name is on the Lord's side of the line and all
> sorrow and disappointment is on the devil's side of the line.
> (George Albert Smith, *Sharing the Gospel with Others*, pp.
> 42-43.)

The warning and counsel of Benjamin is ever fitting: "If ye do not watch yourselves, and your thoughts, and your words, and your deeds, and observe the commandments of God, and continue in the faith of what ye have heard concerning the coming of our Lord, even unto the end of your lives, ye must perish. And now, O man, remember, and perish not." (Mosiah 4:30.)

14

The Spirit Through the Ages

*For the Spirit is the same, yesterday, today, and for-
ever.*

—2 Nephi 2:4

As there is but one Savior, so there is but one gospel, one system of salvation, one plan whereby men can be saved. The gospel
plan is everlastingly the same. If one person who arrives at the age
of accountability must be baptized to enter the kingdom of heaven,
all accountable persons must be baptized to enter that kingdom. If
faith in Christ is required of so much as one man, it is required of
all. If repentance is requisite for salvation in one age among one
people, it is requisite in all ages and among all peoples.

All the principles of the gospel are everlastingly the same. If the
Holy Ghost is available to those of one era, it must be available to
those of all eras. If revelation is available to one man, then it must,
on the same terms, be available to all men. "And thus the Gospel
began to be preached, from the beginning, being declared by holy
angels sent forth from the presence of God, and by his own voice,
and by the gift of the Holy Ghost. And thus all things were confirmed unto Adam, by an holy ordinance, and the Gospel
preached, and a decree sent forth, that it should be in the world,
until the end thereof; and thus it was. Amen." (Moses 5:58-59.)

The Divine Sonship of Christ, and the Holy Ghost

The Book of Mormon provides us with the perfect illustration
that the operations and manifestations of the Spirit are everlastingly the same. Lehi, a man of considerable experience in the
realm of spiritual things, dreamed a dream which he in turn shared
with his family. His older sons, Laman and Lemuel, had hardened
their hearts and thus did not believe the testimony of their father.
However, a younger son, Nephi, believed the words of his father
and sought to obtain the same understanding that had been
granted his father. True to the central theme of the Book of Mormon, Nephi explained that Lehi obtained his understanding because of his "faith on the Son of God," who was the Messiah that
should come (1 Nephi 10:17). Thus Nephi inseparably linked the
principle of revelation and the companionship of the Holy Ghost
with the doctrine of divine sonship. This is because the first and
great revelation that must come to all who would enjoy the spirit of
revelation and the companionship of the Holy Ghost is the eternal
verity that Christ, our Savior, is literally the Son of God. Such is
the testimony with which every gospel dispensation of which we
have record has been opened.

In the dispensation of Adam, the first reference we have to the
heavens being parted and testimony being borne is that of the
angel sent to instruct Adam and Eve. The angel inquired as to why
they offered sacrifices, to which Adam responded, "I know not,
save the Lord commanded me." In response, the angel explained:
"This thing is a similitude of the sacrifice of the *Only Begotten of
the Father,* which is full of grace and truth. Wherefore, thou shalt
do all that thou doest *in the name of the Son, and thou shalt repent and call upon God in the name of the son forevermore. And
in that day the Holy Ghost fell upon Adam, which beareth record
of the Father and the Son, saying: I am the Only Begotten of the
Father from the beginning, henceforth and forever, that as thou
hast fallen thou mayest be redeemed, and all mankind, even as
many as will."* The Holy Ghost now having fallen upon Adam, the
ancient of days "began to prophesy concerning all the families of
the earth" and to testify of the principles of the gospel. (Moses
5:7–10, italics added.)

God taught Adam the law of sacrifice. By obedience to the law of sacrifice Adam obtained an understanding of it. That understanding came, as the understanding of all principles of salvation must, by revelation. The revelation, which came in this instance by the mouth of an angel, announced the doctrine of divine sonship. Adam's sacrificial offering was simply a similitude of the sacrifice the Son of God would make for all who would repent of their sins and seek salvation in his name. Those so doing were to be blessed with the witness and companionship of the Holy Ghost. Thus the first great revelation recorded for Adam's dispensation was that men could be redeemed from the effects of the Fall through the atoning sacrifice of God's Son, which revelation came by the power of the Holy Ghost.

The meridian dispensation, the dispensation of Christ, opened in like manner. First came the angelic announcement to Mary that she was to be the mother of the "Son of the Highest." In response to her question as to how such a thing could be, she was told: "The Holy Ghost shall come upon thee, and the power of the Highest shall overshadow thee: therefore also that holy thing which shall be born of thee shall be called the Son of God" (Luke 1:32-35). As prophesied among the Book of Mormon peoples, "The Son of God cometh upon the face of the earth. And behold, he shall be born of Mary, . . . she being a virgin, a precious and chosen vessel, who shall be overshadowed and conceive by the power of the Holy Ghost, and bring forth a son, yea, even the Son of God." (Alma 7:9-10.)

We mark the beginning of Christ's ministry and the opening of his dispensation at the time of his baptism at the hands of John in the waters of Jordan. It was on this occasion that the heavens were opened and the voice of the Father was heard, saying: "This is my beloved Son, in whom I am well pleased" (Matthew 3:17). Such was the pattern followed in the Americas, where those assembled at the temple in Bountiful heard the voice of the Father saying: "Behold my Beloved Son, in whom I am well pleased, in whom I have glorified my name—hear ye him" (3 Nephi 11:7). And yet again, the Father and the Son appeared to the youthful Joseph Smith in upstate New York in what we have come to call the Sacred Grove, saying: "This is My Beloved Son. Hear Him!" (Joseph Smith—History 1:17.)

It appears that the doctrine of divine sonship is the foundational doctrine of all gospel dispensations. It is the first and great doctrine to which the Holy Ghost bears witness. This explains why the Revelator said that the "testimony of Jesus is the spirit of prophecy" (Revelation 19:10). Nowhere is this doctrine taught with greater plainness than in the Book of Mormon, the book ordained to be the doctrinal foundation of our dispensation, the book ordained to gather Israel from their lost and fallen state. It seems a most natural conclusion that the foundational doctrine of a dispensation ought also be the foundational doctrine of every converted soul within that dispensation. Appropriately, the testimony of the Messiah as the Son of God is the doctrine with which the Book of Mormon is introduced. We return now to Nephi's testimony.

> Having heard all the words of my father, concerning the things which he saw in a vision, and also the things which he spake by the power of the Holy Ghost, *which power he received by faith on the Son of God—and the Son of God was the Messiah who should come—*I, Nephi, was desirous also that I might see, and hear, and know of these things, by the power of the Holy Ghost, which is the gift of God unto all those who diligently seek him, as well in times of old as in the time that he should manifest himself unto the children of men. For he is the same yesterday, to-day, and forever; and the way is prepared for all men from the foundation of the world, if it so be that they repent and come unto him. For he that diligently seeketh shall find; and the mysteries of God shall be unfolded unto them, by the power of the Holy Ghost, as well in these times as in times of old, and as well in times of old as in times to come; wherefore, the course of the Lord is one eternal round. (1 Nephi 10:17–19, italics added.)

Nephi then recounts that as he pondered the words of his father he was caught away in the Spirit of the Lord "into an exceedingly high mountain," where he did indeed "see" and "hear" and come to "know" the things that had been revealed to Lehi. Significantly, that marvelous manifestation began with a view of the tree in his father's dream, followed by a vision of the city of Nazareth and the virgin, Mary. Nephi witnesses that she too was caught away in the Spirit "and after she had been carried away in the Spirit for the space of a time," he said, "the angel spake unto me, saying: Look! And I looked and beheld the virgin again, bearing a child in her arms. And the angel said unto me: Behold the Lamb of God, yea, even the Son of the Eternal Father! Knowest thou the meaning of the tree which thy father saw?" (1 Nephi 11:1–21.)

We place profound importance on the doctrine of divine sonship. There is no salvation in the worship of false gods, no blessings in the adoration of false Christs, no sanctifying effect in profession of false doctrines. The Holy Ghost finds company only with truth, and then only when it is the companion of righteousness. There are great hosts in our modern world who profess Christ as Savior while rejecting him as Lord. They profess salvation in his name while refusing all obligations of heirship. They eschew discipleship, submission, commitment, and obedience. They profess faith without faithfulness. Theirs is a false hope and a false Christ. Such individuals desire justification without sanctification; they seek to sit down with Abraham, Isaac, and Jacob, and yet have come to the wedding feast in unclean garments. The promise to such is that they will be cast into outer darkness to weep and gnash their teeth (Matthew 22:11–13). They have ignored the testimony of the prophets that the Lord's Spirit cannot abide in unclean tabernacles. The Holy Ghost is the sanctifier, and without his companionship a saving knowledge of Christ is impossible (see 1 Corinthians 12:3). To suppose there can be faith in Christ without faithfulness to Christ is a contradiction in terms.

Others in their creedal professions compound the persons of the Father and the Son. Of such traditions, the Lord said that they are all wrong and "all their creeds [are] an abomination in his sight" (Joseph Smith–History 1:19). They declare God to be without body, parts, or passions and by so doing deny his personal nature and his role as the Father of our spirits. This in turn denies our claim to heirship with the Father and thus defeats both the plan and purpose of salvation.

Paul said "no man speaking by the Spirit of God calleth Jesus accursed" (1 Corinthians 12:3). Indeed, no man speaking any untruth can enjoy the companionship of the Holy Ghost. We must believe in the God of the Saints who have preceded us if we are to ex-

ercise the faith they showed, and we must here share the Spirit
known to those Saints if we are someday to share the glory and
honor that is now known to them.

Keys to Understanding Spiritual Things

To understand the Spirit in one age is to understand the Spirit
in all ages. Lehi stated the principle thus: "The Spirit is the same,
yesterday, today, and forever" (2 Nephi 2:4). Indeed, if there were
no absolutes there could be no salvation. The system ordained in
the councils of heaven whereby men are to be saved is predicated
on the following eternal verities:

God does not change. Moroni testified that God was the same
yesterday, today, and forever, that he was without shadow of
changing or variableness, and that should he change he would
cease to be God (Mormon 9:9–19). The reasoning is perfect. By
definition, God possesses the attributes of godliness in their perfection. Should he change in the slightest degree he would cease to be
perfect.

Joseph Smith said that without the knowledge of the change-
less nature of God we could not exercise faith in him "unto life and
salvation." The Prophet reasoned, "Without this, [man] would
not know how soon the mercy of God might change into cruelty,
his long-suffering into rashness, his love into hatred, and in consequence of which doubt man would be incapable of exercising faith
in him, but having the idea that he is unchangeable, man can have
faith in him continually, believing that what he was yesterday he is
to-day, and will be forever." (*Lectures on Faith,* 3:21.)

The gospel is everlastingly the same. Paul said it well: "One
Lord, one faith, one baptism" (Ephesians 4:5). The Lord does not
have a different gospel for those of different nations. The gospel he
delivered to his disciples in Jerusalem and Galilee was the gospel
that he commissioned them to take to those of every nation, kindred, tongue, and people. It is the same gospel that has been restored to us in this day, and it is the same gospel by which Adam,
Enoch, Noah, Abraham, Moses, and the Book of Mormon peoples
worked out their salvation.

The signs that follow believers are the same in all ages of men. Speaking to Joseph Smith the Lord said, "As I said unto mine apostles I say unto you again, that every soul who believeth on your words, and is baptized by water for the remission of sins, shall receive the Holy Ghost. And these signs shall follow them that believe—In my name they shall do many wonderful works; in my name they shall cast out devils; in my name they shall heal the sick; in my name they shall open the eyes of the blind, and unstop the ears of the deaf; and the tongue of the dumb shall speak; and if any man shall administer poison unto them it shall not hurt them; and the poison of a serpent shall not have power to harm them." (D&C 84:64-72.)

Given that God, the gospel, and the fruits of the gospel are the same among all peoples and in all dispensations, it stands to reason that the operations of the Spirit will also be the same. Thus to understand the things of the Spirit in one age is to understand the things of the Spirit in all ages.

Institutional revelation—that revelation that has found a place in the canon of scripture—and personal revelation are received and understood according to the same principles. Let us take the Doctrine and Covenants as our illustration. This compilation of revelations came in a variety of ways, including the ministration of angels, the appearance of the Father and the Son, visions, the voice of the Lord, inspired writings, and "pure intelligence" flowing into the mind of the Prophet. So it is with personal revelations— they may come in a variety of ways. The various revelations in the Doctrine and Covenants did not always come all at once; some came in piecemeal fashion. The greater part of the revelations in the Doctrine and Covenants did not come in a dramatic way (angels, the audible voice of the Lord, etc.) but rather in a quiet and unobtrusive manner, as the Holy Ghost placed thoughts in the Prophet's mind. So it is with personal revelations: most of them will be quiet and unobtrusive, even to the point that they can be ignored if we do not have ears to hear or eyes to see.

As it is one thing to have the book of Isaiah and entirely another to understand it, so it is one thing to have a patriarchal blessing and entirely another to understand it. The requisites for understanding a patriarchal blessing, or personal revelation in any form, are the same as they are for understanding institutional revelation. Indeed, the better we understand one, the better we will understand the other, simply because the principles by which they are understood are the same. In both instances purity and obedience to the laws and ordinances of the gospel are necessary. Without these we have no claim upon the Holy Ghost as a tutor. Both require thought and study. We are all familiar with divine injunctions to study the scriptures but perhaps have failed to realize that they apply to personal revelation as well as that which has been canonized.

The scriptures are our text for understanding personal revelation. It is in the scriptures that we become familiar with the spirit and doctrines of heaven. It is here that we learn to hear and trust the voice of the Good Shepherd. The greatest revelations of our dispensation had their beginning in scriptural study. It was the study of the book of James that led Joseph Smith into the Sacred Grove, the labor of translating the Book of Mormon that led him and Oliver Cowdery to the banks of the Susquehanna where the Aaronic Priesthood was restored, and the study of the book of John that resulted in the vision on the degrees of glory. Joseph Smith received much revelation as a result of scriptural study. As it was with Joseph, so it will be with us, simply because the principles are the same.

All people of all ages have equal need for and a divine entitlement to the blessings of salvation. Given that there is no salvation without revelation, it naturally follows that all people can by compliance with the same principles obtain the same revealed witness. "Not only those who believed after [Christ] came in the meridian of time, in the flesh, but all those from the beginning, even as many as were before he came, who believed in the words of the holy prophets, who spake as they were inspired by the gift of the Holy Ghost, who truly testified of him in all things, should have eternal life, as well as those who should come after, who should believe in the gifts and callings of God by the Holy Ghost, which beareth record of the Father and of the Son; which Father, Son, and Holy Ghost are one God, infinite and eternal, without end" (D&C 20:26–27).

Significantly, the principles of revelation and the role of the Holy Ghost in this life do not differ on the other side of the veil. Those who will yet hear and receive the gospel in the world of the spirits must do, as Peter declared, "according to men in the flesh" (1 Peter 4:6). They must seek and obtain the same spiritual confirmation that would have been required of them had the gospel come to them in this estate. As to the manner in which departed spirits teach the gospel, Nephi tells us that "angels speak by the power of the Holy Ghost; wherefore, they speak the words of Christ" (2 Nephi 32:3).

The knowledge that God, the gospel, and the operations of the Spirit are everlastingly the same enhances our understanding of that which took place anciently, even in instances in which the scriptural text is silent. For instance, since John the Baptist, who traced his keys and authority to Aaron, restored the authority to baptize, we know that they were baptizing in Old Testament times (D&C 84:27). Since Elijah restored the sealing power, thereby enabling those of our dispensation to bind all gospel ordinances on earth and in heaven, we know that the same authority was exercised anciently. When the Lord tells us that he has commanded his Saints in other ages to build temples for the performance of sacred ordinances, we have a meaningful idea of what they were doing (D&C 124:39). We have no keys, powers, authority, or doctrines that have not been restored to us from the faithful Saints of dispensations past.

The Witness of the Spirit Through the Ages

The system by which the gospel of Jesus Christ has been taught throughout the ages had its beginning with father Adam and mother Eve. Having enjoyed an intimate association with God prior to the Fall, they communicated that experience to their children. Thus their children were initially dependent on the testimony of their parents for their knowledge of God. Those of Adam's children who exercised faith in their parents' testimony and obediently observed the ordinances of the gospel obtained the witness of the Spirit and had the heavens opened to them. They thereby became competent witnesses in their own right and thus the spiritual mentors of the rising generation.

Such has ever been the system by which the message of salvation has been declared. Each dispensation has at its head a chosen witness, one to whom the glories of heaven have been revealed. Those susceptible to the whisperings of the Spirit listen to and trust in the words of the initial witness. Through faith and obedience these believers obtain an independent witness of the truths taught by their dispensation head and become the spiritual mentors for the next generation of believers. As the Prophet explained, "It was the credence they gave to the testimony of their fathers, this testimony having aroused their minds to inquire after the knowledge of God; the inquiry frequently terminated, indeed always terminated when rightly pursued, in the most glorious discoveries and eternal certainty" (*Lectures on Faith,* 2:56).

Each generation has its sign seekers, those who taunt the spiritual order, demanding evidence without faith and without obedience. Theirs seems, at least for the moment, a secure position. Were God to show signs to the doubters, he would in so doing reward their doubt and indolence, thus establishing faithlessness and waywardness as legitimate means by which one could obtain the attention and favor of heaven.

Conclusion

The nature of God and the nature of the gospel assure us that the operations of the Spirit will ever be the same. There are no spiritual bargain days, no dispensational absolutions from eternal laws, no winking at the sins of a select or chosen few. As God cannot be God without all attributes of godliness in their perfection, so heaven cannot be heaven if its citizenry are admitted according to varying standards. All who will be saved must be saved by exercising faith in the same God and rendering obedience to the same laws and the same ordinances. In turn they harvest the same fruits of the Spirit, including the companionship of the Holy Ghost, the operations of which have been the same in all ages.

It is and has been the role of the Holy Ghost in all ages to bear witness of the Father and the Son. "This is my doctrine," the resurrected Christ announced to the Nephites, "and it is the doctrine which the Father hath given unto me; and I bear record of the Father, and the Father beareth record of me, *and the Holy Ghost beareth record of the Father and me; and I bear record that the Father commandeth all men, everywhere, to repent and believe in me.*" One cannot have the Holy Ghost while denying that Jesus is the Christ, nor can one have the companionship of the Spirit while denying Christ's testimony of the Father. Where the Holy Ghost is, there the testimony of the Father and the Son is also. Again, Christ said, *"This is my doctrine, and I bear record of it from the Father; and whoso believeth in me believeth in the Father also; and unto him will the Father bear record of me, for he will visit him with fire and with the Holy Ghost."* (3 Nephi 11:32, 35, italics added.)

The text appropriately continues with the affirmation that the Father, the Son, and the Holy Ghost are one. As there is but one gospel or one path that leads to the kingdom of heaven, so there can be only one testimony that comes from the heavens. The Father, the Son, and the Holy Ghost are one, and we, in accepting their testimony, become one with them. Indeed, the doctrine of oneness can properly be said to capsulize the whole system of salvation. We are saved to the extent that we have become one with them. Thus we find Christ saying, "If ye are not one ye are not mine" (D&C 38:27).

Because the operations of the Spirit are everlastingly the same, the scriptures become a timeless textbook on spiritual things. Any and all principles we glean from the scriptures about the operations of the Lord's Spirit are as true of personal revelation as they are of institutional or canonized revelations. Through the scriptures we obtain a familiarity with the Spirit by which we can identify it as it is manifest in our personal affairs.

As the doctrine that opened our dispensation was the testimony that Christ was God's Beloved Son, and as every dispensation of which we have record was opened with that same testimony, we conclude that this must be the foundational doctrine of our own testimonies. This testimony of Christ's divine sonship is inseparable from the companionship of the Holy Ghost.

The system by which the gospel has been taught in all ages is by the mouths of witnesses—chosen vessels who by the power of the Holy Ghost testify with authority of the verities of heaven (see Moroni 7:31). Those trusting their testimony, those who plant the same seeds of faith and obedience in their hearts, are then rewarded with the same harvest as those from whom they received the seeds. They become competent witnesses in their own right and a source of light to others. Thus the power of the gift of the Holy Ghost is passed from one generation to another.

Bibliography

Anderson, Richard L. *Understanding Paul.* Salt Lake City: Deseret Book Co., 1985.

Berrett, William E. "Teaching by the Spirit." In *Charge to Religious Educators.* Salt Lake City: The Church of Jesus Christ of Latter-day Saints, 1981.

Charlesworth, James H., ed. *The Old Testament Pseudepigrapha.* 2 vols. Garden City, New York: Doubleday & Company, Inc., 1983–85.

Clark, J. Reuben, Jr. "The Charted Course of the Church in Education." In *J. Reuben Clark, Selected Papers.* Ed. David H. Yarn. Provo, Utah: Brigham Young University Press, 1984.

Conference Reports of The Church of Jesus Christ of Latter-day Saints. Salt Lake City: The Church of Jesus Christ of Latter-day Saints, October 1910, April 1960, April 1973, October 1973, April 1976, April 1978, October 1981, October 1985.

Eusebius. *Ecclesiastical History.* Grand Rapids, Michigan: Baker Book House, 1977.

Far West Record, Minutes of The Church of Jesus Christ of Latter-day Saints, 1830–1844. Eds. Donald Q. Cannon and Lyndon W. Cook. Salt Lake City: Deseret Book Co., 1983.

Goodspeed, Edgar J. *How Came the Bible?* New York: Abingdon Press, 1940.

Harrison, R. K. *Introduction to the Old Testament.* Grand Rapids, Michigan: Wm. B. Eerdmans Publishing Co., 1969.

Improvement Era 8, no. 7 (May 1905).

Journal History, 23 February 1847. Comp. Andrew Jenson et al. Salt Lake City: Historical Department, The Church of Jesus Christ of Latter-day Saints, 1906.

Journal of Discourses. 26 vols. Liverpool: F. D. Richards & Sons, 1855–86.

Kimball, Spencer W. "Pray Always." *Ensign,* October 1981.

_____. *The Teachings of Spencer W. Kimball.* Ed. Edward L. Kimball. Salt Lake City: Bookcraft, 1982.

Lee, Harold B. *Stand Ye in Holy Places.* Salt Lake City: Deseret Book Co., 1974.

_____. *Ye Are the Light of the World.* Salt Lake City: Deseret Book Co., 1974.

Lundwall, N. B., comp. *Discourses on the Holy Ghost.* Salt Lake City: Bookcraft, 1975.

Madsen, Truman G. "The Olive Press." *Ensign,* December 1982.

Matthews, Robert J. *"A Plainer Translation": Joseph Smith's Translation of the Bible, A History and Commentary.* Provo, Utah: Brigham Young University Press, 1975.

McConkie, Bruce R. Address delivered at BYU First Stake Conference, 11 February 1968.

_____. *Doctrinal New Testament Commentary.* 3 vols. Salt Lake City: Bookcraft, 1965–73.

_____. "The Doctrinal Restoration." In *The Joseph Smith Translation: The Restoration of Plain and Precious Things.* Eds. Monte S. Nyman and Robert L. Millet. Provo, Utah: Religious Studies Center, Brigham Young University, 1985.

_____. "The Foolishness of Teaching." Address to Church Educational System. Salt Lake City: The Church of Jesus Christ of Latter-day Saints, 1981.

_____. "How to Get Personal Revelation." *New Era,* June 1980.

_____. "Jesus Christ and Him Crucified." In *1976 Devotional Speeches of the Year.* Provo, Utah: Brigham Young University Press, 1977.

_____. *Mormon Doctrine.* 2d ed. Salt Lake City: Bookcraft, 1966.

_____. *A New Witness for the Articles of Faith.* Salt Lake City: Deseret Book Co., 1985.

_____. *The Promised Messiah.* Salt Lake City: Deseret Book Co., 1978.

_____. Remarks at the funeral of S. Dilworth Young, 13 July 1981.

_____. "To Honest Truth Seekers." Letter of 1 July 1980.

McConkie, Joseph Fielding. *Gospel Symbolism.* Salt Lake City: Bookcraft, 1985.

_____. *Prophets and Prophecy.* Salt Lake City: Bookcraft, 1988.

McConkie, Joseph Fielding, and Robert L. Millet. *Doctrinal Commentary on the Book of Mormon.* 4 vols. Salt Lake City: Bookcraft, 1987-.

———. *Sustaining and Defending the Faith.* Salt Lake City: Bookcraft, 1985.

McConkie, Oscar W. *The Holy Ghost.* Salt Lake City: Deseret Book Co., 1944.

McKay, David O. *Cherished Experiences.* Comp. Clare Middlemiss. Salt Lake City: Deseret Book Co., 1976.

Messenger and Advocate 1 (October 1834).

Millet, Robert L. *By Grace Are We Saved.* Salt Lake City: Bookcraft, 1989.

Millet, Robert L., and Joseph Fielding McConkie. *In His Holy Name.* Salt Lake City: Bookcraft, 1988.

———. *The Life Beyond.* Salt Lake City: Bookcraft, 1986.

The *New English Bible with the Apocrypha.* New York: Oxford University Press, 1971.

Nibley, Hugh W. *Since Cumorah.* Salt Lake City: Deseret Book Co., 1967.

Packer, Boyd K. *"That All May Be Edified."* Salt Lake City: Bookcraft, 1982.

Pratt, Parley P. *Autobiography of Parley P. Pratt.* Salt Lake City: Deseret Book Co., 1976.

———. *Key to the Science of Theology.* 9th ed. Salt Lake City: Deseret Book Co., 1965.

Roberts, B. H. *The Gospel and Man's Relationship to Deity.* Salt Lake City: Deseret Book Co., 1965.

Shipley, Joseph T. *Dictionary of Word Origins.* New York: Philosophical Library, 1945.

Smith, George Albert. *Sharing the Gospel with Others.* Salt Lake City: Deseret Book Co., 1948.

Smith, Joseph. *History of The Church of Jesus Christ of Latter-day Saints.* 7 vols. Ed. B. H. Roberts. Salt Lake City: Deseret Book Co., 1957.

———. *Lectures on Faith.* Salt Lake City: Deseret Book Co., 1985.

———. *Teachings of the Prophet Joseph Smith.* Comp. Joseph Fielding Smith. Salt Lake City: Deseret Book Co., 1976.

_____. *The Words of Joseph Smith.* Comps. Andrew F. Ehat and Lyndon W. Cook. Provo, Utah: Religious Studies Center, Brigham Young University, 1980.

Smith, Joseph F. *Gospel Doctrine.* Salt Lake City: Deseret Book Co., 1970.

Smith, Joseph Fielding. *Answers to Gospel Questions.* 5 vols. Salt Lake City: Deseret Book Co., 1957–65.

_____. *Doctrines of Salvation.* 3 vols. Comp. Bruce R. McConkie. Salt Lake City: Bookcraft, 1954–56.

Smith, Lucy Mack. *History of Joseph Smith by His Mother.* Salt Lake City: Bookcraft, 1958.

Snow, Eliza R. *Biography and Family Record of Lorenzo Snow.* Salt Lake City: Deseret News Co., 1884.

Times and Seasons. 6 vols. Nauvoo, Illinois: The Church of Jesus Christ of Latter-day Saints, 1839–46.

Tyler, Daniel. Cited in *Juvenile Instructor* 27, no. 93 (1 Feb. 1892):94.

Whitney, Orson F. *Life of Heber C. Kimball.* Salt Lake City: Bookcraft, 1973.

Subject Index

Gratitude, 120
  to God, *xii*, 99
Greek language, 93, 94
Greek philosophy, 2

– H –

Happiness, 11, 14, 49, 86, 87, 99, 149
  celestial, 87
Harris, Martin, 141
Healing, 157
  gift of, 56, 60, 62, 64
Heart, change of, 91, 92, 101
Heaven, 50, 127, 129, 160
  fruits of, 93
Heavenly Father. *See* God
Hebrew language, 74, 94
Helaman (son of Helaman), 129
Holiness, 125, 129, 139–40, 148–49
Holy Ghost, baptism of, 4, 41, 78, 83, 85,
  99, 105, 107, 138
  Christ taught by, 72
  Comforter, 17, 76–88, 116, 130
  companionship of, 33, 51–52, 53
  converter, 120
  gift of, *xi*, 2, 4–8, 35, 39–40, 46–48, 56,
    65, 92, 94, 118, 125, 136–37, 142, 148,
    151, 158, 162
  giving offense to, 140–42
  Holy Spirit of Promise, 70, 105, 123–37,
    139
  impossible to deceive, 124
  nature of, 8
  olive oil a symbol for, 71
  quenching, 142–43
  received by Adam, 152
  reception of, 21, 46
  remission of sins through, 77–79
  sanctifier, 104–11, 155
  sin against, 143–48
  speaking by power of, 57–58
  symbols of, 66–75
  teaching by, 112–22
  understanding through, 82
  withdrawal of, 79, 138–39, 141
Holy Ghost, The (book), 77, 80
Holy Spirit of Promise, 70, 105, 123–37,
  139
Hope, 85, 108, 133
"How to Get Personal Revelation"
  (article), 19

Humility, 39, 116, 132
Hyde, Orson, on sanctification, 105
Hymns, 60
Hypocrisy, 20, 39, 81

– I –

In His Holy Name (book), 83, 103, 145
Intellect, 114
Intelligence, 16–17, 157
Isaiah, book of, 157
  on righteousness, 49
Israel, gathering of, 90, 154

– J –

Jacob (son of Lehi), on excessive zeal, 32
  on quenching the Spirit, 140
James, book of, 158
  on wisdom from above, 41, 49
Jeremiah, on a new covenant, 131–32
Jerusalem, 156
Jesus Christ, 9, 20, 47, 79, 119, 140, 142,
  151
  acceptance of, 21–22
  adoption into family of, 93
  "anointed one," 71–72
  apostles of, 74
  appearance to Joseph Smith, 1, 24, 33
  appearances, 130, 157
  atonement, 77–79, 104, 147, 153
  betrayal of, 148
  baptism of, 66, 153
  change through, 100
  Comforter promised by, 17, 76
  hope in, 85
  instructions to Nicodemus, 93
  Light of, 6–8, 43–44, 125, 138–41
  love of, 85–86
  love for children, 50
  Nephite ministry, 84, 161
  on being born again, 90
  on blasphemy against the Holy Ghost,
    144
  on building on a sandy foundation, 28
  on entering the rest of God, 124
  on sanctification, 106, 109
  on teaching by the Spirit, 113–14
  on those born of the Spirit, 74
  on two comforters, 130
  parable of the mustard seed, 15–16

Scripture Index

OLD TESTAMENT

NEW TESTAMENT

BOOK OF MORMON

DOCTRINE AND COVENANTS

PEARL OF GREAT PRICE